San Rafael High School District

185 Mission Avenue
San Rafael, CA 94901

W9-BUP-362

HOLISTIC MEDICINE

GENERAL EDITORS

Dale C. Garell, M.D.
Medical Director, California Childrens Services, Department of Health
  Services, County of Los Angeles
Clinical Professor, Department of Pediatrics & Family Medicine,
  University of Southern California School of Medicine
Associate Visiting Professor, Maternal & Child Health, School of Public
  Health, University of Hawaii
Former president, Society for Adolescent Medicine

Solomon H. Snyder, M.D.
Distinguished Service Professor of Neuroscience, Pharmacology, and
  Psychiatry, Johns Hopkins University School of Medicine
Former president, Society of Neuroscience
Albert Lasker Award in Medical Research, 1978

CONSULTING EDITORS

Robert W. Blum, M.D., Ph.D.
Associate Professor, School of Public Health and Department of
  Pediatrics
Director, Adolescent Health Program, University of Minnesota

Charles E. Irwin, Jr., M.D.
Associate Professor of Pediatrics, Division of Adolescent Medicine,
  University of California, San Francisco

Lloyd J. Kolbe, Ph.D.
Chief, Office of School Health & Special Projects, Center for Health
  Promotion & Education, Centers for Disease Control

Jordan J. Popkin
Director, Division of Federal Employee Occupational Health, U.S. Public
  Health Service

Joseph L. Rauh, M.D.
Professor of Pediatrics and Medicine, Adolescent Medicine, Children's
  Hospital Medical Center, Cincinnati

THE ENCYCLOPEDIA OF
H E A L T H

MEDICAL ISSUES

DALE C. GARELL, M.D. · GENERAL EDITOR

HOLISTIC MEDICINE

James S. Gordon, M.D.

Introduction by C. Everett Koop, M.D., Sc.D.

Surgeon General, U.S. Public Health Service

(95) T 48515

San Rafael High School Library
185 Mission Avenue
San Rafael, CA 94901

CHELSEA HOUSE PUBLISHERS

New York · Philadelphia

6/3
Gor

•   •   •   •   •   •   •

The goal of the ENCYCLOPEDIA OF HEALTH *is to provide general information in the ever-changing areas of physiology, psychology, and related medical issues. The titles in this series are not intended to take the place of the professional advice of a physician or other health-care professional.*

ON THE COVER a computer-generated adaptation of an anatomical drawing by Leonardo da Vinci

Chelsea House Publishers
EDITOR-IN-CHIEF: Nancy Toff
EXECUTIVE EDITOR: Remmel T. Nunn
MANAGING EDITOR: Karyn Gullen Browne
COPY CHIEF: Juliann Barbato
PICTURE EDITOR: Adrian G. Allen
ART DIRECTOR: Giannella Garrett
MANUFACTURING MANAGER: Gerald Levine

The Encyclopedia of Health
SENIOR EDITOR: Jane Larkin Crain

Staff for HOLISTIC MEDICINE
ASSOCIATE EDITOR: Paula Edelson
COPY EDITOR: David Waldstreicher
DEPUTY COPY CHIEF: Ellen Scordato
EDITORIAL ASSISTANTS: Nicole Bowen, Susan DeRosa
PICTURE RESEARCHER: Debra P. Hershkowitz
DESIGN: Debby Jay, Jean Weiss
DESIGNER: Victoria Tomaselli
ASSISTANT DESIGNER: Donna Sinisgalli
PRODUCTION COORDINATOR: Joseph Romano

Copyright © 1988 by Chelsea House Publishers, a division of Main Line Book Co. All rights reserved. Printed and bound in the United States of America.

3 5 7 9 8 6 4

Library of Congress Cataloging in Publication Data
Gordon, James S. (James Samuel)
  Holistic medicine.

  (The Encyclopedia of Health)
  Bibliography: p.
  Summary: Defines holistic medicine and discusses its treatment of the patient, its use in practice, and its future in health care.
  1. Holistic medicine—Juvenile literature.
  [1. Holistic medicine] I. Title. II. Series.
  R733.G67 1988   613   88-6039
  ISBN 0-7910-0522-4 (pbk.)

CONTENTS

THE ENCYCLOPEDIA OF
H E A L T H

PREVENTION AND EDUCATION: THE KEYS TO GOOD HEALTH

C. Everett Koop, M.D., Sc.D.
Surgeon General,
U.S. Public Health Service

The issue of health education has received particular attention in recent years because of the presence of AIDS in the news. But our response to this particular tragedy points up a number of broader issues that doctors, public health officials, educators, and the public face. In particular, it points up the necessity for sound health education for citizens of all ages.

Over the past 25 years this country has been able to bring about dramatic declines in the death rates for heart disease, stroke, accidents, and, for people under the age of 45, cancer. Today, Americans generally eat better and take better care of themselves than ever before. Thus, with the help of modern science and technology, they have a better chance of surviving serious—even catastrophic—illnesses. That's the good news.

But, like every phonograph record, there's a flip side, and one with special significance for young adults. According to a report issued in 1979 by Dr. Julius Richmond, my predecessor as Surgeon General, Americans aged 15 to 24 had a higher death rate in 1979 than they did 20 years earlier. The causes: violent death and injury, alcohol and drug abuse, unwanted pregnancies, and sexually transmitted diseases. Adolescents are particularly vulnerable, because they are beginning to explore their own sexuality and perhaps to experiment with drugs. The need for educating young people is critical, and the price of neglect is high.

Yet even for the population as a whole, our health is still far from what it could be. Why? A 1974 Canadian government report attrib-

7

uted all death and disease to four broad elements: inadequacies in the health-care system, behavioral factors or unhealthy life-styles, environmental hazards, and human biological factors.

To be sure, there are diseases that are still beyond the control of even our advanced medical knowledge and techniques. And despite yearnings that are as old as the human race itself, there is no "fountain of youth" to ward off aging and death. Still, there is a solution to many of the problems that undermine sound health. In a word, that solution is prevention. Prevention, which includes health promotion and education, saves lives, improves the quality of life, and, in the long run, saves money.

In the United States, organized public health activities and preventive medicine have a long history. Important milestones include the improvement of sanitary procedures and the development of pasteurized milk in the late 19th century, and the introduction in the mid-20th century of effective vaccines against polio, measles, German measles, mumps, and other once-rampant diseases. Internationally, organized public health efforts began on a wide-scale basis with the International Sanitary Conference of 1851, to which 12 nations sent representatives. The World Health Organization, founded in 1948, continues these efforts under the aegis of the United Nations, with particular emphasis on combatting communicable diseases and the training of health-care workers.

But despite these accomplishments, much remains to be done in the field of prevention. For too long, we have had a medical care system that is science- and technology-based, focused, essentially, on illness and mortality. It is now patently obvious that both the social and the economic costs of such a system are becoming insupportable.

Implementing prevention—and its corollaries, health education and promotion—is the job of several groups of people:

First, the medical and scientific professions need to continue basic scientific research, and here we are making considerable progress. But increased concern with prevention will also have a decided impact on how primary-care doctors practice medicine. With a shift to health-based rather than morbidity-based medicine, the role of the "new physician" will include a healthy dose of patient education.

Second, practitioners of the social and behavioral sciences—psychologists, economists, city planners—along with lawyers, business leaders, and government officials—must solve the practical and ethical dilemmas confronting us: poverty, crime, civil rights, literacy, education, employment, housing, sanitation, environmental protection, health care delivery systems, and so forth. All of these issues affect public health.

Third is the public at large. We'll consider that very important group in a moment.

Fourth, and the linchpin in this effort, is the public health profession—doctors, epidemiologists, teachers—who must harness the professional expertise of the first two groups and the common sense and cooperation of the third, the public. They must define the problems statistically and qualitatively and then help us set priorities for finding the solutions.

To a very large extent, improving those statistics is the responsibility of every individual. So let's consider more specifically what the role of the individual should be and why health education is so important to that role. First, and most obviously, individuals can protect themselves from illness and injury and thus minimize their need for professional medical care. They can eat a nutritious diet, get adequate exercise, avoid tobacco, alcohol, and drugs, and take prudent steps to avoid accidents. The proverbial "apple a day keeps the doctor away" is not so far from the truth, after all.

Second, individuals should actively participate in their own medical care. They should schedule regular medical and dental checkups. Should they develop an illness or injury, they should know when to treat themselves and when to seek professional help. To gain the maximum benefit from any medical treatment that they do require, individuals must become partners in that treatment. For instance, they should understand the effects and side effects of medications. I counsel young physicians that there is no such thing as too much information when talking with patients. But the corollary is the patient must know enough about the nuts and bolts of the healing process to understand what the doctor is telling him. That is at least partially the patient's responsibility.

Education is equally necessary for us to understand the ethical and public policy issues in health care today. Sometimes individuals will encounter these issues in making decisions about their own treatment or that of family members. Other citizens may encounter them as jurors in medical malpractice cases. But we all become involved, indirectly, when we elect our public officials, from school board members to the president. Should surrogate parenting be legal? To what extent is drug testing desirable, legal, or necessary? Should there be public funding for family planning, hospitals, various types of medical research, and medical care for the indigent? How should we allocate scant technological resources, such as kidney dialysis and organ transplants? What is the proper role of government in protecting the rights of patients?

What are the broad goals of public health in the United States today? In 1980, the Public Health Service issued a report aptly entitled *Promoting Health-Preventing Disease: Objectives for the Nation.* This report expressed its goals in terms of mortality and in terms of intermediate goals in education and health improvement. It identified 15 major concerns: controlling high blood pressure; improving family planning; improving pregnancy care and infant health; increasing the rate of immunization; controlling sexually transmitted diseases; controlling the presence of toxic agents and radiation in the environment; improving occupational safety and health; preventing accidents; promoting water fluoridation and dental health; controlling infectious diseases; decreasing smoking; decreasing alcohol and drug abuse; improving nutrition; promoting physical fitness and exercise; and controlling stress and violent behavior.

For healthy adolescents and young adults (ages 15 to 24), the specific goal was a 20% reduction in deaths, with a special focus on motor vehicle injuries and alcohol and drug abuse. For adults (ages 25 to 64), the aim was 25% fewer deaths, with a concentration on heart attacks, strokes, and cancers.

Smoking is perhaps the best example of how individual behavior can have a direct impact on health. Today cigarette smoking is recognized as the most important single preventable cause of death in our society. It is responsible for more cancers and more cancer deaths than any other known agent; is a prime risk factor for heart and blood vessel disease, chronic bronchitis, and emphysema; and is a frequent cause of complications in pregnancies and of babies born prematurely, underweight, or with potentially fatal respiratory and cardiovascular problems.

Since the release of the Surgeon General's first report on smoking in 1964, the proportion of adult smokers has declined substantially, from 43% in 1965 to 30.5% in 1985. Since 1965, 37 million people have quit smoking. Although there is still much work to be done if we are to become a "smoke-free society," it is heartening to note that public health and public education efforts—such as warnings on cigarette packages and bans on broadcast advertising—have already had significant effects.

In 1835, Alexis de Tocqueville, a French visitor to America, wrote, "In America the passion for physical well-being is general." Today, as then, health and fitness are front-page items. But with the greater scientific and technological resources now available to us, we are in a far stronger position to make good health care available to everyone. And with the greater technological threats to us as we approach the 21st century, the need to do so is more urgent than ever before. Comprehensive information about basic biology, preventive medicine, medical and surgical treatments, and related ethical and public policy issues can help you arm yourself with the knowledge you need to be healthy throughout your life.

FOREWORD

Dale C. Garell, M.D.

Advances in our understanding of health and disease during the 20th century have been truly remarkable. Indeed, it could be argued that modern health care is one of the greatest accomplishments in all of human history. In the early 1900s, improvements in sanitation, water treatment, and sewage disposal reduced death rates and increased longevity. Previously untreatable illnesses can now be managed with antibiotics, immunizations, and modern surgical techniques. Discoveries in the fields of immunology, genetic diagnosis, and organ transplantation are revolutionizing the prevention and treatment of disease. Modern medicine is even making inroads against cancer and heart disease, two of the leading causes of death in the United States.

Although there is much to be proud of, medicine continues to face enormous challenges. Science has vanquished diseases such as smallpox and polio, but new killers, most notably AIDS, confront us. Moreover, we now victimize ourselves with what some have called "diseases of choice," or those brought on by drug and alcohol abuse, bad eating habits, and mismanagement of the stresses and strains of contemporary life. The very technology that is doing so much to prolong life has brought with it previously unimaginable ethical dilemmas related to issues of death and dying. The rising cost of health-care is a matter of central concern to us all. And violence in the form of automobile accidents, homicide, and suicide remain the major killers of young adults.

In the past, most people were content to leave health care and medical treatment in the hands of professionals. But since the 1960s, the consumer of medical care—that is, the patient—has assumed an increasingly central role in the management of his or her own health. There has also been a new emphasis placed on prevention: People are recognizing that their own actions can help prevent many of the conditions that have caused death and disease in the past. This accounts for the growing commitment to good nutrition and regular exercise, for the fact that more and more people are choosing not to smoke, and for a new moderation in people's drinking habits.

People want to know more about themselves and their own health. They are curious about their body: its anatomy, physiology, and biochemistry. They want to keep up with rapidly evolving medical technologies and procedures. They are willing to educate themselves about common disorders and diseases so that they can be full partners in their own health-care.

The ENCYCLOPEDIA OF HEALTH is designed to provide the basic knowledge that readers will need if they are to take significant responsibility for their own health. It is also meant to serve as a frame of reference for further study and exploration. The ENCYCLOPEDIA is divided into five subsections: The Healthy Body; The Life Cycle; Medical Disorders & Their Treatment; Psychological Disorders & Their Treatment; and Medical Issues. For each topic covered by the ENCYCLOPEDIA, we present the essential facts about the relevant biology; the symptoms, diagnosis, and treatment of common diseases and disorders; and ways in which you can prevent or reduce the severity of health problems when that is possible. The ENCYCLOPEDIA also projects what may lie ahead in the way of future treatment or prevention strategies.

The broad range of topics and issues covered in the ENCYCLOPEDIA reflects the fact that human health encompasses physical, psychological, social, environmental, and spiritual well-being. Just as the mind and the body are inextricably linked, so, too, is the individual an integral part of the wider world that comprises his or her family, society, and environment. To discuss health in its broadest aspect it is necessary to explore the many ways in which it is connected to such fields as law, social science, public policy, economics, and even religion. And so, the ENCYCLOPEDIA is meant to be a bridge between science, medical technology, the world at large, and you. I hope that it will inspire you to pursue in greater depth particular areas of interest, and that you will take advantage of the suggestions for further reading and the lists of resources and organizations that can provide additional information.

•   •   •   •

· · · · · · · · · · · · · · ·

THE HOLISTIC
APPROACH TO
HEALING

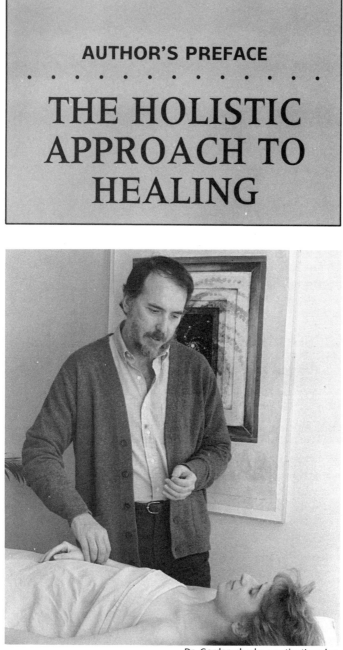

Dr. Gordon checks a patient's pulse.

When we graduated from Harvard Medical School in 1967, most of my classmates and I moved confidently forward into our specialty and subspecialty training, focusing on the latest physiological or pharmacological advances in our particular areas of interest. I was, if not typical, at least on the bell curve for that year's aspiring psychiatrists. I had considered becoming a surgeon like my father, or a general practitioner like my grandfather. I liked the idea of taking care of families over many years. But my real pleasure, I discovered, was in talking to people, in exploring their inner worlds, in understanding and helping them to understand the connections between their life histories and their illnesses.

At the time of my graduation, I was prepared to believe that there was an important distinction between physical and mental illness. The former, although influenced by emotions, was basically physiological, whereas "mental" illness was, with few exceptions, psychological and social.

Over the next 10 years I worked in and outside of mental hospitals. I was a chief resident in psychiatry at the Albert Einstein College of Medicine, and then a research psychiatrist at the National Institute of Mental Health. I was particularly interested in the way individual and social attitudes affected the definition and treatment of people with emotional problems. And I worked to create therapeutic communities in which troubled teenagers could learn to see their individual emotional problems as part of a healthy process of growth and development. I was also seeing private patients, adults as well as teenagers. My professional life seemed very much in order. People were respectfully reading what I was writing. I was becoming an expert in the treatment of troubled adolescents and their families.

Yet something was beginning to nag at me. It was obvious that just as psychological and social factors could affect physical health, so biological factors could affect psychosocial functioning. What really bothered me, I realized, was the biological therapies we had developed to treat aspects of "mental" illnesses. Too often, it seemed, such treatments violated the thoughts and feelings of our patients, or relieved one set of biological problems only to create side effects (weight gain; palpitations; serious, sometimes irreversible tremors, etc;) that troubled and sometimes disabled patients. And yet there were biological aspects to mental illness.

Perhaps, I reasoned, one could view biological symptoms, like psychological symptoms, as clues to the origins of the disturbance, and as opportunities for growth and change. Perhaps patients could, with our help, discover and use nontoxic remedies that could treat physical problems, just as psychotherapy and the therapeutic community could treat psychological and social problems.

I cast about for possible therapeutic strategies, and discovered excerpts from Chinese scientific journals about the successful and widespread use of acupuncture analgesia in major surgery, and the treatment by acupuncture of anxiety, schizophrenia, osteoarthritis, and bronchial asthma. Chinese medicine, I read, conceived of the physical and mental as two aspects of one embracing system of energy, which could be affected by food, exercise, and counseling as well as acupuncture. This integral approach appealed to me, but still I found the claims for acupuncture hard to believe. I thought its success might simply be a placebo response (the result of patients' positive expectations and their esteem for the practitioner). But my prejudice lessened when I discovered that this ancient technique was being successfully used in veterinary medicine. Here, I thought hopefully, was an apparently effective, nontoxic, biologically based healing practice that I might use to help people with psychological problems.

About two years after I began to read about acupuncture, I injured my lower back. The doctor I saw prescribed muscle relaxants, bed rest, and exercises, but these did not alleviate the problem, and the specialists who were called in were baffled. Still in a considerable amount of pain, and feeling (I confess) far more sympathetic toward patients I had seen who had described vague symptoms that fit no particular diagnosis, I called an osteopath who was trained in acupuncture and whom I had met by chance two years earlier. His recommendations—a diet of nothing but pineapple and hot baths with Epsom salts together with manipulation of my spine and acupuncture—seemed absurd to say the least, but to my surprise and gratification it figured prominently in my recovery.

This experience turned my mild curiosity about alternative healing techniques and the holistic approach to medicine into a kind of fascination. I have since learned that acupuncture, which I now practice, can indeed be useful in the treatment of physical and psychological problems. I have studied and currently practice musculoskeletal manipulation, which works to affect the spinal column; hypnosis, which I have used to treat physical as well as psychological problems; yoga and meditation; and nutritional therapies, which have been proven to be essential to the functioning of both mind and body.

I have incorporated these techniques in an effort to create a truly holistic practice that includes both orthodox and alternative therapies. What I try to stress to my patients is that the holistic approach is not simply a group of alternative therapies or a new specialty, but rather an informed return to what is best and most enduring in medicine, and the beginning of a new synthesis of contemporary medicine and the larger healing tradition of which it is but a part.

•   •   •   •

CHAPTER 1

· · · · · · · · · · · · · · · ·

WHAT IS HOLISTIC MEDICINE?

An engraving depicting the ancient Greek holistic healer Hippocrates.

Since the early 1970s, the adjective "holistic" (derived from the ancient Greek *holos*, meaning "whole") has been revived and applied to almost every human endeavor from jogging to home building. This is not surprising. The belief that our society and its functions are becoming increasingly fragmented and specialized is widespread. At a time when narrow perspectives and single solutions appear inadequate to our problems, holism has emerged as an alternative, a catchall for our hopes.

The idea of holism, and the word itself, were first introduced by the South African statesman and biologist Jan Christiaan Smuts in his 1926 book, *Holism and Evolution.* To Smuts, holism was a way of viewing and describing living things, including people, as entities greater than and different from the sum of their parts. It was also an antidote to a scientific approach that attempts to understand all phenomena, including human beings, by reducing them to their most basic biological processes.

The practice of medicine, that curious hybrid of art and science that affects all our lives so intimately, has been particularly influenced by science and technology and the pressures toward reduction and specialization. In recent years, it has also become the most fertile ground for the development of a holistic perspective and practice.

There have been some major scientific achievements in the 20th century, an era that has witnessed the development of such crucial antibiotics as penicillin for the treatment or control of many previously fatal diseases. Unfortunately, these advances

Penicillin mold in a nutrient solution. One of the major discoveries of 20th-century medicine, penicillin can cure such serious diseases as scarlet fever and bacterial pneumonia. Unfortunately, it is not an effective treatment for many stress-related conditions.

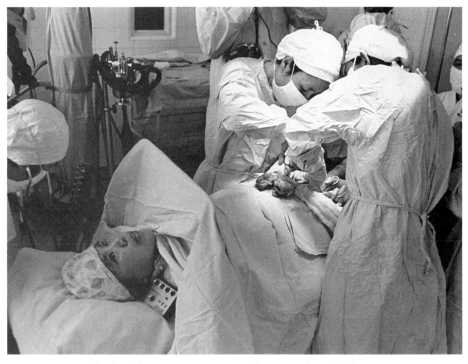

A woman anesthetized by acupuncture remains conscious during a cesarean delivery in a Beijing, China, hospital. This ancient techinique is becoming a popular form of anesthesia among holistic surgeons.

have not produced definitive cures for many common stress-related conditions, such as high blood pressure, depression, alcoholism, and insomnia. In addition, there are a great many people who feel that the focus of modern Western medicine is too impersonal and too narrow; those who share this belief stress that many doctors tend to view their patients as biological machines rather than human beings.

Holistic medicine is an alternative to this type of medical approach. It does not neglect the need for swift and sophisticated medical or surgical action, but does emphasize health promotion and patient education. In doing so, it respects the capacity people have for healing themselves and regards them as active partners in health care rather than passive recipients.

In addition to including the use of modern technology and medicines, holistic medicine welcomes all of the techniques that have been developed in other cultures and at other times. A holistically oriented surgeon may use 5,000-year-old acupuncture to provide anesthesia for the most technologically sophisticated microsurgery. A holistic oncologist (cancer specialist) may rely on computer-assisted X rays to locate a malignant tumor and then call on the power of the patient's faith and imagination to help reduce the size of that tumor.

The holistic approach to medicine includes *humanistic* medicine, which emphasizes the relationship between physicians and patients, and the psychological and spiritual development of both the patient and physician; *psychosomatic* medicine, which is concerned with the interdependence and mutual influence of psychological and physical factors; and *behavioral* medicine, which stresses the psychological and social causes and effects of illness.

Holism has always been vital to healing, and some of history's most gifted physicians have embraced holistic beliefs. The ancient Greek physician Hippocrates, writing in the 5th century B.C., emphasized the environmental causes and treatment of illness, and the importance of emotional factors and nutrition in health and disease. He spoke at length of the wisdom of the healing force of nature and of the physician's need to use it. Similarly, Chinese and Indian texts reveal the importance that these ancient healing traditions placed on the maintenance of harmony between the individual and the social and natural world, on diet, exercise and meditation, self-care, and self-regulation. Holistic medicine has been described by its critics as being a specialty, like surgery or oncology, or a collection of such untraditional (for the Western world) techniques as acupuncture or chiropractic. In fact, it is a synthesis that may include and integrate all of these. It can be described as a marriage of the art of healing that has been so vital to medicine throughout history, and the scientific precision of modern medicine. Perhaps most important, it may well represent a significant advance, not only in our health care but in the way we live and think and feel about ourselves.

HOLISM AND WHOLISM

Sometimes holistic is written "wholistic." This emphasizes the importance of the approach to the "whole" person and in addition substitutes the more familiar English word for the one that is derived from Greek. Some writers suggest that "wholistic medicine" emphasizes the spiritual aspects of health care—for example, the meaning each illness may have in the unfolding of the whole of our lives and the lessons we can learn from it. But others have thought that "holistic" highlights these aspects. There is, in fact, no real difference between the words. "Holistic" is the spelling most people prefer, and for that reason will be used in this book.

HOLISTIC HEALTH AND HOLISTIC MEDICINE

People often speak of holistic health and holistic medicine as if they were interchangeable. This is only partly true. The holistic attitude and approach, the respectfulness, comprehensiveness, and open-mindedness are the same. But holistic medicine is the application of this approach by physicians who have trained as M.D.s (medical doctors) or D.O.s (doctors of osteopathy), whereas holistic health is the approach to health care taken by nonphysician health-care providers— nurses, psychologists, counselors, physical and massage therapists, nutritionists, chiropractors, and so on, or by patients themselves.

A man assumes a yoga posture. The stretching and bending exercises of yoga are deeply relaxing and can also lower blood pressure.

HOLISTIC MEDICINE, SELF-CARE, AND WELLNESS

Since the 1970s, the "self-care" and "wellness" movements have grown together with holistic medicine. Although they are in many ways related and have exerted a beneficial mutual influence on each other, the emphases are different.

Self-care refers to the care that people can provide for themselves. It emphasizes the individual's capacity for taking responsibility for his or her care and may include such standard diagnostic and therapeutic procedures as taking one's own blood pressure and reducing salt intake in order to lower blood pressure as well as using the healing techniques of other cultures (for example, doing the bending and stretching exercises of yoga to increase flexibility, produce relaxation, and lower blood pressure).

Wellness is a concept first popularized by Dr. John Travis, who established the first "wellness center" in California in the mid-1970s. Travis was careful to distinguish the treatment of disease from the promotion of wellness. The latter he believed was an educational, rather than a medical, function. Wellness emphasizes teaching people how to change their attitudes and their behavior so they can feel as well as possible. It does not treat their illnesses.

Although there are specific distinctions among self-care, wellness, and holistic medicine, this book will use holistic medicine as a term that may include the others. A holistic physician is someone who is concerned with promoting wellness through educational means and encouraging self-care, as well as with treating illness.

•   •   •   •

Chapter 2

. . . .

A CHANGING WORLD

ALLAN SCHNEIDER, M.D.
DISEASES OF THE
KIDNEY, BLADDER & PROSTATE

DANIEL S. ARICK, M.D.
EAR, NOSE & THROAT
HEAD & NECK SURGERY

TOOMAS M. SORRA, M.D.
GASTROENTEROLOGY
DISEASES OF THE STOMACH,
LIVER, GALL BLADDER & INTESTINES

Holistic medicine has gained a tremendous amount of influence in recent years; although not universal in acceptance, the beliefs behind the holistic approach have come to represent the consensus thinking of many. In order to understand the practice of this type of medicine, it is important first to examine the reasons for this rather dramatic development. This chapter will first discuss some of the larger changes in science and society that provided the context for the development of holistic medicine. It will then explain the evolutionary forces within medicine and health care that gave rise to the perspective that is now called holistic.

The Consumer Rights Movement

The success of the civil rights movement, which during the 1950s and 1960s was crucial to the establishment of laws banning discrimination against black people, provided a lesson that other groups quickly learned. In rapid succession women, the elderly, Hispanics, homosexuals, the handicapped, and many others organized to demand equal rights.

The consumer rights movement was intimately related to and in many ways overlapped these movements. Consumer activists insisted they had the right to full knowledge about the government and corporate policies that affected them, the products they bought, and the services they received.

Soon this consumer consciousness carried over to health-care settings. For example, women who had become aware of discrimination against them also began to recognize the insulting way they were sometimes treated by their male physicians. They

A Canadian paper factory deposits its waste into a river. The problem of pollution helped to galvanize the ecology movement, which stresses the unhealthy consequences that technological exploitation has had upon air, land, and water.

no longer accepted it when their doctors called them "honey," or told them that they need not worry about a surgical procedure, or the side effects of drugs that were prescribed. Women wanted to know what was going on in their bodies and what they could do about it. And they demanded to be treated as thinking, feeling adults by their doctors.

The Ecology Movement

During the 1970s, many people adopted a significantly different way of looking at the relationship between human beings and their environment. Until that time the dominant and largely unquestioned belief was that the natural world was something to be subdued and exploited for personal gain and social and economic well-being. There was a sense, particularly in the United States, that natural resources, such as food, minerals, and energy sources, were all but inexhaustible.

By the mid-1970s, however, it had become clear that the consequences of unlimited growth and exploitation of the environment—the rapid disappearance of natural gas and the equally rapid emergence of dangerously polluted air and water, depleted soils, and despoiled forests—threatened not only the way of life these natural resources had made possible, but our well-being and indeed our survival. It was becoming clear too that the side effects of unbridled technological exploitation were connected and cumulative: Damage done by air pollution in one part of the country could become, as particles were transported by winds, damage to water, soil, wildlife, and vegetation hundreds or thousands of miles away.

The ecology movement of the 1970s insisted that we begin to conserve rather than exploit. We had to learn to restrain our appetites and adapt to the limitations of the natural world rather than continue to try to force it to accommodate to our desires. Ecologists told us that if we developed a new attitude toward nature—one of loving stewardship rather than of selfish exploitation—we might also create a new attitude toward ourselves.

Advances in Psychology and Psychiatry

Although they originated outside of orthodox medicine, some of the new psychological perspectives of the 1960s and 1970s challenged and influenced both the diagnostic and therapeutic procedures of medicine. Two of the most important were family therapy and humanistic psychology. Both had their roots in the late 1950s, became prominent in the United States in the late 1960s, and have since become major influences on both psychotherapy and holistic medicine.

Family Therapy Family therapy involves a way of understanding people as well as a method for helping them. Individual psychology, which has its origins in 19th-century biology, seeks to understand the growth and development of one person, stressing how past experiences shape his or her present actions. Family therapy, which has its intellectual origins in systems theory, conceives of the family as a dynamic system and is particularly concerned with the kinds of interactions that take place within that system. Family therapists focus on the present interactions among family members and how each person fits into the unique pattern of his or her own family unit. They do not see mental illness as a disease existing in one member, but as the expression in one person of problems that are a result of the entire family's poor functioning.

The individual therapist works with one person to increase that person's self-understanding, bring out buried emotions, or to help him or her develop strategies for changing patterns of behavior. The family therapist sees the whole family, points out what is going on among its members, and then acts to change their behavior. For example, a family therapist may sit between parents and the child they continually criticize. This will deflect the parents' focus from the child they are criticizing and force them to face the conflicts between themselves that they want to ignore. It is difficult to pinpoint one specific founder of family therapy, but important pioneers of this form of psychology were Nathan Ackerman and John Spiegal in New York, and Don Jackson and Virginia Satir in California.

Humanistic Psychology Humanistic psychology was named by Abraham Maslow, a research psychologist at Brandeis University in the 1950s. It was, he said, a "third force" in psychology. Maslow felt that the "first force"—Freud's psychoanalysis, which was then the dominant form of psychiatry—was too narrow and pessimistic. It focused on each person's illness, not on his or her capacity for health. Freud believed that psychoanalysis, which is a process of exploring in detail the roots of adolescent and adult

A girl enjoys a game of Chinese checkers with her parents. Family therapists view the family as a system and believe that the health and happiness of each member depend on the well-being of the whole.

problems in the traumatic emotional experiences of childhood, would be therapeutic. But it appears that by "therapeutic," he meant only the exchanging of neurotic misery for ordinary unhappiness.

According to Maslow, the "second force"—behaviorism, which explained human activity as the sum of responses to stimuli—was superficial and reductive. Maslow admitted that its strategies for helping people change their behavior (for example, treating a phobia, or fear, of snakes by devising a series of steps in which one came gradually closer to a snake, first in pictures, then in fact) might be useful. But, he insisted, there was much more to people than their problems, and more to psychology than techniques for solving problems.

Each human being, Maslow said, proceeds through an individual evolutionary development. Once basic needs are met, people naturally want to realize their "higher needs." Humanistic psychology would not only help people deal with their conflicts but would provide guidance for those who wanted to experience the creativity, joy, and love that are the hallmarks of what Maslow called "self-actualization."

From the 1960s on, this enlarged therapeutic perspective was linked with both the ecology and consumer movements. Here is a rough sketch of some of these connections: Individuals are part of the natural world. Each of us is embarked on a journey toward self-actualization, which will in turn be affected by the journeys of all others. This journey may be frustrated by difficulties in individual development and family functioning, by social disorganization, and by environmental destruction. This frustration may create physical, emotional, and spiritual problems. People whose journeys are halted can be helped to see the path to self-actualization if they are treated in a way that fosters their capacity for responsibility, respects their individual rights, and encourages them to become the integral creative part of the natural and social world that they have the potential to be.

A Perceived Crisis in Modern Medicine

New ways of understanding individuals and their relationships to the social and natural world have been important in the development of holistic medicine. But there would never have been much pressure for change in medicine if modern medicine itself were not undergoing what many experts—holistic and nonholistic alike—would call a crisis.

There are five major reasons for this so-called crisis: the historical reevaluation of the benefits of modern medicine; the increase of chronic stress-related illness; the limitations and harmful side effects of the drugs and procedures used in scientific medicine; specialization and the consequent erosion of doctor-patient relationships; and the rapidly rising costs of health care.

The Historical Reevaluation   Until the late 1950s, medical history was perceived as a kind of war in which science, freed from superstition, was steadily advancing on its archenemy, disease. There were wonderful battles fought along the way: In the 1920s the purification of insulin made it possible for diabetics to control their disease; antibiotics capable of destroying previously deadly bacteria were developed in the 1940s and 1950s; each year new surgical procedures capable of saving the lives of young children and prolonging those of older people were developed. In the United States people were living longer than ever before, and almost every year their life expectancy was increasing.

The first significant challenge to this rosy picture came from René Dubos, a microbiologist who helped develop some of the most powerful antibiotics. In his 1959 book, *Mirage of Health*, Dubos drew on published research to suggest that the discoveries that he and others had made had far less to do with improving the health of people in industrialized countries such as the United States than did a variety of economic, social, nutritional, and behavioral advances.

During the next 10 years medical historians began to fill out the picture that Dubos had sketched. In 1976, Thomas McKeown tried to put the differences between medical and nonmedical advances into numbers. He carefully studied public health statistics from England and Wales that had accumulated since the 17th century and concluded that only 10% of the improvement in the death rate from such infectious diseases as tuberculosis and pneumonia could be traced to individual medical treatments

A young potter at her craft. One hallmark of what humanistic psychologists call "self-actualization" is the spontaneous joy that results from doing something creative.

The microbiologist Rene Dubos was a pioneer in the development of antibiotics. He later came to believe, however, that social and behavioral factors are more important to health improvement than medication is.

including antibiotics. Ninety percent of the improvements, he discovered, were due to positive changes in nutrition (better food and farming methods), in the environment (especially the regulation of food and water), and in our behavior (here he singled out population control). As did others who made similar studies, McKeown concluded that the next series of major advances in health would likewise come from changes in diet, behavior, and the environment.

The Increase in Chronic Diseases Since 1900 there has been a major shift in the advanced industrialized countries in the pattern of illness from acute, infectious diseases to chronic stress-related illnesses. This is connected partly to the medical and nonmedical advances discussed above and partly to our increased longevity (the longer people live, the more likely they are to fall ill). But chronic illness is also something we have brought on ourselves as individuals and as a society.

It has been proven that the foods we eat can affect mood and behavior, and that eating natural foods is much more healthy to both mind and body than eating foods with additives. Yet many of us eat meat that has been injected with hormones and antibiotics, and grains and vegetables that have been raised on fields repeatedly sprayed with poisonous pesticides and herbicides. Many food companies process the fiber and nutrients out of their products and put in additives to make the food tastier and give it a longer life on the supermarket shelves.

In addition, many of us lead sedentary lives and do not get enough exercise. We are often besieged by an incredible variety of stimuli: the pressures of job or school; divorces between couples and moves from community to community; grim or uncertain news from all over the world in our newspapers and on television; and great and constant noise. All of these forces tax our physical and emotional capabilities. All these and many more are sources of "wear and tear" on the individual, of stress.

Stress affects people in many different ways and to different degrees, depending on individual differences and prior medical history. One man suffering a significant amount of stress—say fatigue, overeating, problems with his work or his wife—may develop high blood pressure, whereas another experiencing the same problems may have back pain. But both of the men are suffering from stress-related illnesses. When these illnesses per-

A hot dog and soft drink may be tasty, but in the long run foods without additives and refined sugar are much more healthy to mind and body.

Experts agree that such sources of stress as crowded, noisy places can cause chronic physical problems as well as severe anxiety.

sist over a long time or recur periodically they are called chronic or chronic stress-related illnesses.

Studies done in the 1970s have affirmed that stress can be a factor in most of the illnesses that afflict and kill Americans. One such study, done in 1974 and sponsored by the Rockefeller Foundation, revealed that some 50% of the deaths in the United States could be attributed to cardiovascular and cerebrovascular diseases—high blood pressure, heart attacks, and strokes—and 19% to cancer. Stress has been implicated as a factor in all of these conditions. The study went on to detail other stress-related problems: 24 million Americans experience chronic insomnia—about the same number suffer from high blood pressure; up to 50 million people have regular headaches; and perhaps 75 million weigh at least 20 pounds more than they should. A 1978 report by President Carter's Commission on Mental Health added the astonishing facts that some 9 million Americans are alcoholics and "15 percent of our population needs some form of mental health services."

The Limitations and Side Effects of Medical and Surgical Treatments Stress-related illness has proved extremely difficult to treat by conventional medical and surgical means. For example, some cancers can be cured by surgery, radiation, and chemotherapy, but many cannot; sleeping pills can relieve insomnia for a while but in time the individual may become tolerant of or resistant to the medication; antibiotics might kill one type of bacteria but they also may create the climate in which others, often more difficult to destroy, can flourish. In many cases, drugs or surgery may relieve symptoms, but leave the underlying problems untouched.

In addition, many of these treatments were being dangerously overused. A study authorized by the U.S. Congress in 1976 revealed that 2.4 million *unnecessary* operations were performed in 1974 and that 11,900 lives were lost from these procedures. Also during the early 1970s, many physicians were overprescribing dangerous drugs in attempts to reduce their patients' stress. During this time some 5 to 7 million tablets and capsules of Valium and Librium—potentially addictive tranquilizers—were prescribed each year in the United States alone.

Even when used in accordance with accepted practice, medical and surgical treatments were increasingly likely to have serious, lasting, and sometimes irreversible side-effects. In the 1970s the antibiotic chloramphenicol was implicated in the sudden deaths of children who had been treated for infections. Twenty years

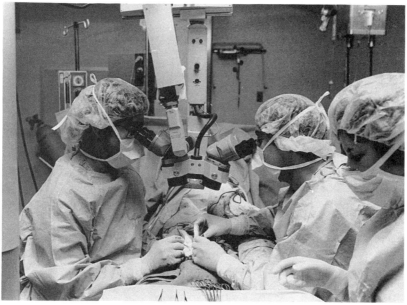

According to one congressional study, surgeons performed more than 2 million unnecessary operations in 1974.

after they were first used, the major tranquilizers that helped reduce the symptoms of people with such serious mental illnesses as schizophrenia were discovered to create sometimes irreversible tremors and rigidity in some patients. Even a nonprescription standby such as aspirin could be a source of dangerous bleeding in the stomach and small intestine.

The Deteriorating Physician-Patient Relationship The occasional ineffectiveness and inappropriate use of drugs and surgery, and their dangerous side effects even when used correctly, all contributed to patients' apprehension about their physicians' knowledge and skill and an erosion of the doctor-patient relationship. But other factors were also at work.

In the early 20th century the vast majority of physicians were general practitioners. They knew and cared for their patients throughout their lives, delivered their children, made house calls, and cared for them at home when they were dying. The physician was a trusted friend as well as an expert on diagnosing and treating disease.

Seventy years later general practitioners are a minority. Most physicians are specialists. They see their patients only at particular times in their lives. Pediatricians take care of them when they are children and specialists in internal medicine treat them when they are adults; obstetricians are called in to deliver their babies. There are even more limitations within these categories. The vast amount of new information, the technical difficulty of many diagnostic and therapeutic procedures, and the prestige and money that come with being an expert have created an incredible variety of specialists and subspecialists.

A man who has bronchitis might first go to a general practitioner, but if the bronchitis becomes pneumonia he might be sent to an internist. If the pneumonia becomes worse, then an infectious-disease specialist is called in. If an abscess develops in the lung the surgeon is summoned. And, as the joke goes, if the patient becomes agitated by his illness, by the bewildering procession of doctors with whom he has to deal, or by the bill he receives, then of course it is time for the psychiatrist.

The situation has not been a comical one for patients. Not only do they see each specialist less often and less consistently than they did the general practitioner of old, but when they see the specialist, it is often only for a few minutes. By the 1970s more and more patients were complaining of being treated "like an object" by doctors who seemed interested only in their disease—not in their patients' feelings.

At the same time doctors were also feeling the ill effects of this system. It was most obvious when they themselves became patients and were subjected to the same type of assembly-line treatment. But many also began to feel bitter and dissatisfied with their work. They did not have the close, satisfying relationships with patients that many of them had hoped to find. It seemed to them that if patients were treated like pieces of machinery to be repaired and reassembled, they were turning into highly paid assembly-line workers.

This was most obvious in some prepaid health programs in the United States and in National Health Service plans in Europe, where doctors had to see a certain number of patients each hour, but it was also increasingly true of doctors in private practice in the United States. The consequence of physician dissatisfaction could be read in the far higher-than-average rates of alcoholism, drug addiction, and suicide among them.

One of the unfortunate consequences of western medicine's ever-increasing sophistication and specialization is that the once-common house call has become virtually obsolete.

The Ever Higher Cost of Medicine All of the factors discussed above have contributed to the crisis in modern medicine and the emergence of holistic medicine. But in the long run it may well be the ever-increasing cost of health care that will promote the spread of the holistic approach.

In 1977, the total expenses for a health-care system that was clearly not meeting the needs or effectively treating the illnesses of the U.S. population was $162.6 billion dollars, or 8.8% of a Gross National Product in which health care was the single largest item. And each year the cost of health care increased at twice the rate of all other costs. In the late 1980s, health care makes up more than 11% of the Gross National Product.

All the other factors that have been discussed—both within and outside the medical care system—have paved the way for holistic medicine, creating a social, moral, and intellectual climate in which a holistic approach seems right. The changes in patterns of illness, shortcomings in treatment methods, and inadequacies in the way treatment has been offered have combined to make some other approach—at once more appropriate, effective, and humane—necessary. The enormous cost of providing care that does not meet our needs makes change increasingly attractive if not inevitable.

•   •   •   •

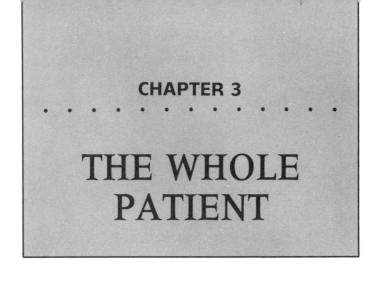

CHAPTER 3

· · · · · · · · · · · · · · · ·

THE WHOLE
PATIENT

The dissatisfaction with mainstream medicine described in the previous chapter was very much "in the air" in the United States, Canada, and Western Europe in the 1970s. Parts of it appeared in print in journals of medicine, health, and public policy. Some of it was argued persuasively in books with self-explanatory titles, such as the social philosopher Ivan Illich's *Medical Nemesis* and Rick Carlson's *The End of Medicine*. Most of it was present in whole or part in the understanding of those physicians who became leaders in the soon-to-be-born field of holistic medicine.

Family therapy has proven to be an effective treatment for tension and stress that occur as a result of dysfunctions within the family.

Many of these doctors, myself included, were clinicians—people who cared for sick patients every day—and often researchers as well. For us the statistics of chronic illness and the side effects of drugs were made immediate by the very real suffering of patients with heart disease and cancer, arthritis and allergies, back pain and headaches, depression, and other forms of mental illness.

Every day we saw patients who were not getting well in spite of the best available medical and surgical treatment, given by the most conscientious physicians. We frequently observed the negative side effects of therapeutic drugs: medication that decreased blood pressure but also caused exhaustion, depression, and sexual impotence; tranquilizers given to teenagers that made them feel less anxious but undermined their ability to concentrate and to learn; antibiotics that successfully treated bladder infections in women but also led to the development of vaginal yeast infections. And increasingly, many patients complained that the very doctors who were unable to help them dismissed their problems as "all in your head" and refused to pay attention to the emotional aspects of their patients' illnesses.

The physicians who witnessed these happenings were all motivated by some particular combination of intellectual curiosity and professional and personal experience to move beyond the medical model we were taught and to explore new possibilities. Many of us were certified in medical specialties such as psychiatry, internal medicine, gynecology, and surgery. In time we developed, each of us in our own way, a new perspective on the ancient practice of medicine—the holistic approach.

This chapter will discuss three aspects of this approach. These categories, which are vital to the foundations of holistic medicine, can be described as comprehensiveness, uniqueness, and transformation. Each implies a viewpoint that includes professional and personal experiences and has very real practical consequences.

The Comprehensiveness of Holistic Medicine

Holistic medicine understands that we are biochemical, physiological, emotional, mental, and spiritual beings. We are part of a family and society; we have roles we play at work and at home. We are citizens of a nation and inhabitants of the earth. And we are always changing.

This comprehensive view suggests that health and illness depend on maintenance of all these functions and relationships. It also means that when one or another of these aspects of life is disturbed others may be affected. Finally it suggests to the holistic physician that he or she may treat patients on any or all of these levels at once or separately.

In practice this means that a person may have an inherited chance of developing a particular physical problem but that the immediate cause of that problem may be an event or a situation on a different level. For example, the end product of asthma is spasms of the smooth muscles surrounding the bronchial tree,

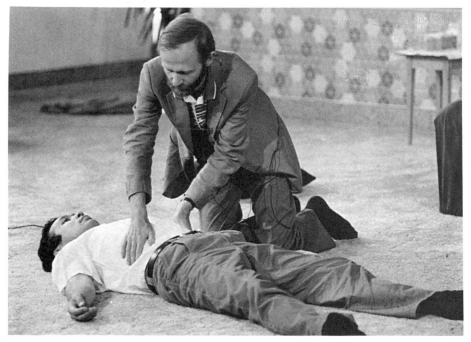

A boy learns a slow-deep-breathing technique. Holistic physicians often recommend this or other relaxation methods as an alternative to tranquilizers in the treatment of anxiety.

which in turn causes difficulty in breathing. But a holistic approach will search for causes at all different levels. The triggering event may be a psychological feeling of being smothered or abandoned by others; a family situation that seems so restrictive that it feels "hard to breathe"; a job that makes a person want to cry but is difficult to give up.

A holistic physician will try to find out which situations trigger the attacks and why, for example, the upcoming visit home or a meeting with the boss is particularly stressful. The answers to these and other questions will dictate the kinds of changes and therapies he or she suggests. If the stress occurs in the context of family relations, family therapy may be the treatment of choice. If the job is a major problem, then he or she may suggest discussions with the boss; if that does not help a change in employment may be necessary.

The holistic physician may use medication—inhalers or pills or injections of adrenaline—in a life-threatening or a seriously debilitating situation, but the emphasis will be on the long-term improvement of functioning without medication. In any case the patient will be taught some kind of relaxation technique, perhaps slow deep breathing to decrease the likelihood of an attack while anticipating or going through the stressful situation. Changes in patterns of exercise may be prescribed to strengthen lung functioning. Foods that may stress the system, such as sugar and caffeine, can be removed from the patient's diet. Allergy-causing substances that affect the lungs may also be identified and proscribed.

Important psychological influences are often involved in the case of asthma and most other chronic illnesses. Sometimes a holistic physician who is not a psychiatrist may refer an anxious or depressed asthma patient to a psychiatrist or other mental-health professional. Other times it may be easier for the patient to talk to the physician he or she knows and trusts.

For many people seeing a mental-health professional still carries with it a sense of shame. The emphasis that many traditional psychiatrists place on early childhood as the root of all emotional problems may clash with the patient's belief that his or her problems are physical or result from the present situation. The holistic physician has a more flexible approach and is therefore more able to work within the patient's own way of looking at the world. He or she can emphasize those strategies—physical changes and alternative ways of coping with present problems, as well as past traumas and family patterns—that are most appropriate to the patient's situation and way of thinking.

The Uniqueness of Each Patient

The previous discussion has focused on the different strategies the holistic physician may adopt in the treatment of a particular patient. The specifics of this approach will differ with each patient and each physician and, from time to time, with the same patient and physician. This is because each patient is unique.

Many people believe that the idea of uniqueness has largely been removed from the thinking of modern medicine. It has been argued that the emphasis of modern medical training is—except at times in psychiatry—on statistical norms and predictable outcomes. For example, a given percentage of patients who suffer from a particular illness recover from it. A particular sequence of treatments is followed for virtually all those who have a particular diagnosis, and an average dose of medication per pound of body weight prescribed. Individual differences among patients are largely ignored, with the exception of the one-in-a-million diagnosis, the "interesting case."

The holistic perspective, by contrast, tells us that every case is unique. The "garden-variety pneumonia" that may bore the average internist fascinates the holistic physician because he or she sees each pneumonia as being as different, as full of mysteries to be appreciated and understood as the unique person who has the illness. The bacteria that produce pneumonia in two people who are under stress (and therefore may be more susceptible to infection) may be the same. The same antibiotics may be used to treat them. But the physician may approach each case differently. One man may be susceptible to pneumonia because he is avoiding a job he hates. Another has been working too hard to complete a project he loves. The first man may have to be helped to find different work, lest in an effort to avoid his situation, he makes himself ill again. The second may have to be counseled to slow down, lest he be unable to do what he loves.

This sense of uniqueness is firmly grounded in biology. Each of us has a different genetic makeup; each of us has different fingerprints; thus, we do not have the same biological makeup.

The biochemist and nutritionist Roger Williams, who discovered pantothenic acid, one of the B vitamins, has spent a considerable part of his career focusing on this issue. Williams says that everyone has his or her own "biochemical individuality," which is as unique as a fingerprint. According to his research, our requirements for vitamins, minerals, and other nutrients may vary by as much as 1,000 times from one person to another.

The implications of this biochemical individuality are far-reaching. The "average daily requirement" of a vitamin as determined by the U.S. Department of Agriculture may be more than enough for one person and far too little for another. Similarly, a dose of medication that may be inadequate for one person may be dangerously toxic to another, even though the two people are statistically identical (that is, both are of the same age and weight and in the same general state of health).

Their focus on the uniqueness of each patient has led holistic physicians to another area of interest that until the 1970s was

Bernie Siegel, a Yale Medical School surgeon, has formed groups of "exceptional patients," in which people help each other discover their own unique reasons for living and getting well.

largely neglected by medicine: the "exceptional patient." Previously, people who recovered from illnesses that should have killed them—for example, patients who survived a cancer that had spread to most of their body—were put in the category of "spontaneous remission." They were regarded as curiosities, but only of passing interest.

Since the mid-1970s holistic physicians and psychologists have become fascinated by the concept of spontaneous remission, by people who somehow beat the overwhelming odds against them. What, the investigators have begun to ask, makes these people live or recover faster from illnesses whereas so many others languish or die? The answers, still incomplete, seem to include a tremendous desire to live—for some purpose, for another person, or because of a fighting spirit or a sense of joy.

Because these qualities seem to be therapeutic, holistic physicians have tried to find ways to discover and promote them in their patients. Many of them work with patients individually, but others, such as Bernie Siegel, a Yale Medical School surgeon and author of the best-selling *Love, Medicine and Miracles*, have formed groups of "exceptional patients" in which people can help one another to discover their own unique reasons for living and getting well.

Healing as a Transformational Process

The interest in exceptional patients is connected with the spiritual side of holistic medicine. In much of the ancient world, illness was regarded as a spiritual as well as a physical and emotional crisis. It signified that the individual had somehow strayed from the path that God or Nature or the Great Spirit had decreed. One task of the healer (known among other things as the medicine man, witch doctor, or shaman) was to help the lost person find his or her way—to provide spiritual guidance as well as medical care. In this way, the priestly and medical functions were generally combined in one person, the priest-physician.

This perspective, which may seem strange to us now, was very much a part of Western medicine until the late Middle Ages. From that time on the separation of the religious and the medical function became more and more distinct. The physician cared for the body and mind; the priest or minister or rabbi attended to the soul. Each kept a distance from the other.

By the 1970s a significant challenge to this division was under way. It had been sparked by a wider knowledge of the ways that the spiritual and medical functions are united in other cultures and by our growing appreciation of the wisdom of our ancestors who saw illness as a spiritual crisis. But it was confirmed by the daily practice of physicians who found themselves trying to make sense out of illnesses that seemed to arise, and sometimes to disappear, for no obvious reason. And it was reinforced by the growing knowledge and experience with exceptional patients.

When holistic physicians began to ask their patients why they became ill, and whether or not they would get better, they found that often enough the patients had very definite ideas. To the first question many responded that they were at a "dead end" in their lives, or at a "turning point" that they felt they could not navigate. Illness was a way out, a retreat. Others declared, directly or through symbolic drawings, that they felt overwhelmed by their illness or that they did not believe they deserved to live.

Instead of simply filing this information away or trying to convince their patients to change their minds, many holistic physicians stood it on its head. Although illness could be seen as a misfortune, even a calamity, it could also be viewed as an opportunity. We reminded ourselves and our patients that the Chinese written character for "crisis" is the same as the one for "opportunity." If we and our patients looked at illness as an opportunity for growth, a signal from the body and mind that the person's whole life was not going as it should, then perhaps a profoundly beneficial change was possible.

For many people this proved to be the case. Instead of remaining victims of their illness they became its students. This in itself helped them to overcome the feelings of helplessness and

Former Saturday Review *editor Norman Cousins claims that he was able to overcome a progressive joint disease called ankylosing spondylitis through laughter, optimism, and a sense that he was in control of his own treatment.*

hopelessness that are sometimes major contributors to early death or prolonged illness. With the help of their physicians, they investigated the reasons why they became ill and tried to find the path to self-actualization that illness had interrupted. If patients could discover this path, they could view illness as a part of life, a catalyst in a process of ongoing transformation.

•   •   •   •

CHAPTER 4

· · · · · · · · · · · · · ·

THE PATIENT AS PARTNER

For many years the ideal picture of a doctor-patient relationship was composed of a white-coated, handsome older man
leaning solicitously toward an obviously anxious patient. The
doctor, kindly and wise, dispensed reassuring advice or medicines, ordered tests, and readied himself to perform procedures.
The patient was silent, passive, trusting.

Since the early 1970s a number of elements in this picture
have changed. Patients, once silent and worshipful, uninformed

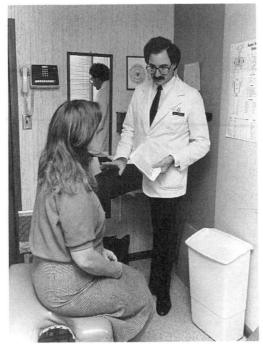

The relationship between doctor and patient is a crucial part of holistic treatment. The physician will often enlist the patient's help in diagnosing the ailment and prescribing a treatment.

and trusting, have become increasingly well informed about health and illness and are increasingly vocal and challenging in their dealings with their physicians. Patients now may interview several physicians before they select one. When a procedure is recommended they may demand to know why this particular one has been selected. What is the evidence for its effectiveness, they ask, and can you show me copies of the research papers on which it is based?

The response to this new informed assertiveness has been mixed. Some doctors resent the challenges to their authority. Others accept them gracefully. Holistic physicians generally welcome them. From the holistic physician's point of view an informed and active patient, one who is willing to take responsibility for him or herself, is crucial to successful health care.

From the first session holistic physicians try to engage their patients in every aspect of the diagnostic and therapeutic practice. They will encourage their patients to search for the origins of their illness in their present life situation. "Why do you think you became ill at this time?" and "What does your illness mean to you?" are two of the questions I often pose. By asking them the physician not only gains valuable information but encourages his or her patients to be active partners in diagnosing—literally "seeing through"—their problems.

The same principle applies when it comes to treatment. Of course in some instances patients are unaware of their options. In the case of many chronic illnesses, however, they are in fact experts on what types of treatment work for them. Still, when a holistic physician asks people what they think they should do, patients are often incredulous: "That's what I came here to find out." But when physicians persist, they often come up with treatment plans that are remarkably like the ones their doctors would have devised for them. They know the kinds of changes they should make. "My diet's all wrong"; "I'm taking too much medication"; "I need time to myself." The physician can then help them find ways to make the changes that they sense are necessary.

In this way the doctor is changing the situation from a telling to a teaching one. Instead of laying down the law to the patient, the doctor helps the patient find his or her own way. When the two parties do agree on a particular treatment regimen—reduction or elimination of previously prescribed drugs, exercise, diet changes, relaxation techniques—it is not a command that must be obeyed without argument, but a collaborative adventure in which they have decided to participate.

TREATMENT WITHOUT MEDICATION

Although holistic physicians may use drugs and surgery, and do so when they are indicated, most of them prefer to use techniques that do not have dangerous side effects, do not cause dependence, and are capable of being administered and controlled by the patients themselves. This method of treatment can also help the patient bring about lasting changes that will not only help cure current problems but also prevent future ones.

Self-Regulation Strategies

Techniques for self-regulation include relaxation therapies, hypnosis, biofeedback, guided imagery, and meditation. Some of these techniques can be used in highly sophisticated and specific ways. Others are quite simple and straightforward. One or another of them can be taught to patients by an experienced practitioner in a brief period of time. All are based on the ability of the mind to control the body and many of its functions, and all involve the mind's capacity to produce relaxation.

Relaxation is defined as a generalized lowering of the level of physiological arousal. That is, it is a state in which the heartbeat and respiratory rates are slow, blood pressure is low, and brain activity is dominated by alpha waves. This type of brain wave is characterized by a frequency of 8 to 11 waves per second and denotes a kind of alert calm. Muscles are relaxed, hands and feet are warm, and stress is low.

Relaxation Therapies Relaxation therapies are the simplest of the self-regulatory techniques. A very popular one, called "progressive muscular relaxation," was developed by Dr. Edmund Jacobson in the 1930s. It involves contraction and then relaxation of all the muscle groups in the body, beginning with the feet and extending upward to include legs, pelvis, stomach, back, chest,

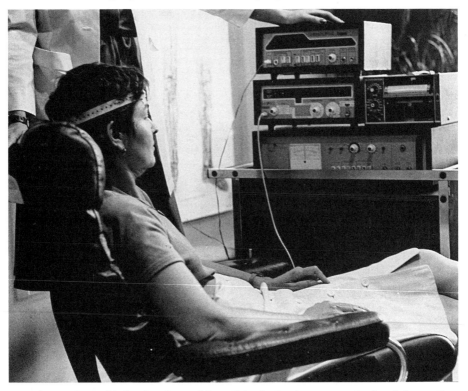

A patient using a biofeedback machine. This device issues continuing information about specific biological functions—such as heart rate—so that the patient can learn to control them.

arms, neck, and head. The practitioner tenses the muscles on inhalation and relaxes them on exhalation. The contraction and relaxation may be accompanied by a phrase of autosuggestion ("self"-suggestion) such as "I am" (inhale/contract muscles) "relaxed" (exhale/relax muscles).

Biofeedback Biofeedback refers to the feedback of information about biological processes and is based on the idea that people who are given information about their body's internal processes can use this information to learn to control these processes. For example, a subject who is presented with continuous information about the fluctuations of temperature in his or her hands (through a sensor attached to his or her finger that displays the temperature on a screen) can learn to raise or lower his or her own temperature. In a similar way individuals can use information about their heart rate and brain waves to alter and control them.

Biofeedback can be used not only to lower a person's general stress level, but also in specific clinical situations. For example, many people with severe and debilitating migraine headaches seem to suffer a general constriction of their arteries as well. By learning to warm her fingertips, a woman can relax the muscles in the walls of her arteries throughout the body and obtain relief from her pain and discomfort.

Hypnosis Hypnosis comes from hypnos, the Greek word for "sleep," but it actually seems to be a combination of relaxation and increased alertness and suggestibility. This hypnotic or "trance" state can be induced by a hypnotist's tone of voice, repetitive stimulation as by a pendulum or metronome, or even by the mind-boggling confusion induced by a long and baffling story. Individuals can also hypnotize themselves by using a repetitive stimulus or by listening to a tape of the hypnotist's or their own voice in which instructions are given to relax, let go, and enter the characteristic state.

One of the most striking uses of hypnosis is for pain reduction. In the 19th century, before anesthesia was widely available, the Scottish physician James Esdaille used hypnosis to produce analgesia (a pain-free state) in more than 3,000 operations. Now hypnosis may be used to reduce pain in such chronic illnesses as migraine headaches and arthritis, as well as in childbirth.

Other therapeutic uses of hypnosis rely on the individual's capacity to use the hypnotic trance to explore previous experiences and alter present states. For example, hypnosis can be used to regress a person to the age at which he or she first developed a phobia. In the hypnotic state the traumatic situation that produced the phobia may be reexperienced and alternative solutions may be suggested: A boy who is afraid of going to sleep may trace his fear to arguments that his parents had around bedtime. The hypnotist may then suggest, while the boy is still in a trance, that his parents will not harm each other and that he will see them alive and well in the morning.

Hypnosis can also be used as a technique for substituting beneficial physical responses for destructive ones: The overweight patient who continually feels hungry may be instructed under hypnosis to breathe deeply instead of reaching for food when the hunger arises.

Guided Imagery Guided imagery is probably a form of hypnosis. In it particular mental images are used to alter the body and mind in a therapeutic way. Guided imagery may simply be used to produce relaxation, as when someone is instructed to imagine that he or she is in a beautiful peaceful place under a warm sun. It can also be made very specific. For example, physicians Carl Simonton and his wife, Stephanie Matthews Simonton, discovered that guided imagery could be used to improve the immune response of some cancer patients. They instructed these patients to imagine their white blood cells—representatives of the body's immune system—attacking and destroying their tumor cells. And they found that these images were followed by actual increases in white blood cells. Similarly, depressed people can use images to picture themselves in happier circumstances, and thereby improve their mood.

In addition, guided imagery is used by holistic physicians as an aid to diagnosis and in planning therapy. A depressed woman may be told to see herself in a peaceful place. Once she seems relaxed she may be asked to imagine that she is meeting someone very wise who is able to help her understand what her problem is. When this creature—some people conjure up a wise old man or woman or a clever talking animal—appears in the fantasy, he, she, or it often has valuable answers. These explanations, which are sometimes funny and unexpected as well as helpful, seem to come from some intuitive part of the patient's unconscious mind to which the process of guided imagery permits access.

Chickens and other livestock are often fed hormones to make them grow larger, but such additives make them far less healthy foods.

Meditation Meditation is sometimes used as a synonym for relaxation. But although both states may produce lower blood pressure and a greater feeling of calm, meditation differs in essence from both relaxation and hypnosis. Meditation is a state of relaxation and alertness—one in which the meditator may exercise great control over physiological processes—but it is not a particularly suggestible state. In fact, the meditator has a kind of independence, a calm detached acceptance that sets him or her apart from people who are relaxed or hypnotized.

Indeed, one can see other self-regulatory strategies as preparations for meditation, rather than its equivalent. Relaxation, guided imagery, biofeedback, and hypnosis are all therapeutic techniques, ways that have been devised for coping with and improving physical and mental functioning. The meditative state, by contrast, is one in which the meditator instinctively "knows" what is disturbing the body and mind: This "knowing," furthermore, can actually begin a process of *resolving* the disturbance. The Indian spiritual teacher J. Krishnamurti said of this state:

"Seeing is solving." In fact meditation is closer to religious experience than therapeutic practice. The Bible speaks of "the peace that passeth understanding." Finally, the meditative state is extremely difficult to put into words. Perhaps it is best to leave the explanation to the Chinese sage Lao-Tzu, who observed, "The way that can be described is not the way."

FOOD AND NUTRITION

Twenty-five hundred years ago Hippocrates told his students to "let food be your medicine and medicine your food." For many years, modern medicine ignored this directive. Nutrition, except in the context of such severe deficiency diseases as scurvy and rickets (vitamin C and vitamin D deficiencies), which were rarely seen in the United States, was not even discussed. Conventional medical wisdom maintained that as long as an individual obtained enough calories and enough foods from the "four basic food groups" (meat, milk, fruits and vegetables, and grains), adequate nutrition and adequate vitamins and minerals were as-

Allergies are often caused by wheat and dairy products and can sometimes be controlled if these foods are removed from the diet.

sured. During the last 15 years holistic physicians, nutritionists, and lay people have challenged this perspective and returned to Hippocrates' advice.

Because the quantity of information about nutrition is vast, and conclusive evidence for the efficacy of one or another diet is rare, there are only a few principles, and a few generally agreed upon facts to discuss. To begin with, the diet that most of us have been eating for the last 30 years is totally different from the one that characterized our species for the previous 30,000 years. It is composed of far more animal fats, refined sugars, and salt, as well as processed and preserved substances. There is far less bulk, fiber, and raw food in our diet. There are food additives, some of which are themselves toxic or carcinogenic (cancer producing). Much of what we eat has been raised in soil polluted by herbicides and pesticides. In addition, meat and poultry may have been contaminated by the antibiotics, hormones, and other chemicals designed to make animals grow larger.

This diet tends to promote the development of a host of chronic diseases, including high blood pressure, arthritis, and inflammations of the large intestine (colitis) and small intestine (ileitis). It overworks the pancreas and adrenal gland, which control sugar metabolism, and may be implicated in some cases of depression, anxiety, and childhood "hyperactivity." In addition, it seems likely that our diet has contributed in a major way to the food allergies that have become well recognized in recent years.

A holistic approach to medicine inevitably involves altering the modern diet in the direction of the way that human beings ate for tens of thousands of years. Holistic physicians, however, differ among themselves about the exact composition of the proper diet. Some might favor predominantly raw foods, for example. Others rely on the *macrobiotic* (literally, "great life") diet, which closely resembles the traditional Japanese fare of brown rice, vegetables, and fish, and which some people believe can help prevent the development of many chronic diseases.

Although many physicians are skeptical of the claims put forward by proponents of raw food and macrobiotics, most would agree with the recommendations of the Senate Select Committee on Nutrition. The "dietary goals" that the committee announced in 1977 were strongly influenced by holistic practitioners and are currently endorsed by virtually all physicians. They include recommendations to reduce the amounts of fats (particularly animal fats), cholesterol, sugar, and salt, and to increase the amount of complex carbohydrates (grains and beans). Coupled with an emphasis on whole grains rather than refined flour and the avoidance of preserved and processed food (which have additives and are often depleted of nutrients), such a diet may well help prevent or retard the development of chronic diseases and will be conducive to maintaining an optimum body weight.

Food Elimination In addition to these general dietary goals, many holistic physicians have become interested in food elimination. This may involve both fasting (abstinence from all but one or several foods for a period of time) and elimination of foods to which a patient is believed to be particularly sensitive. The most common fasts are with distilled water, quantities of one fruit, or fruit or vegetable juices. Fasts may range from one day to several weeks. This procedure, which is part of virtually all of the world's healing traditions, is meant to give the body a rest from the work of digesting, assimilating, and eliminating food and to facilitate the elimination of toxic substances that have accumulated in the cells during periods of "normal eating."

Although there is no literature on the efficacy of fasting in Western scientific journals, it is a subject of intensive study in Eastern Europe and the Soviet Union. Fasts are widely used throughout the world and are widely reported to produce feelings of increased energy and well-being. It is very important to note, however, that they should be attempted only with a physician's guidance.

It has long been known that some people are allergic to certain foods: A man eats broccoli and immediately breaks out in hives. A woman eats soft-shell crabs and experiences severe stomach pains. In recent years holistic physicians have become interested in the less obvious "hidden food allergies." These conditions, which seem to have increased dramatically with the increase in processed, preserved, and chemically contaminated food, do not become obvious until one stops eating the offending food for a while. Then if one eats it, the symptoms appear. This is particularly important, because hidden allergies may be implicated in a variety of chronic illnesses including, among others, arthritis, asthma, eczema, and depression.

To discover a hidden allergy a holistic physician may do blood

Nobel Prize winner Linus Pauling conducted several studies concerning the preventative and therapeutic use of vitamin C for several ailments ranging from the common cold to cancer.

tests to determine which foods are involved. Alternatively, suspected foods can be withdrawn for a period of time and then reintroduced. If, for example, the symptoms decrease when wheat or milk (two common hidden allergens) are withdrawn and then reappear when a dairy or wheat meal is given, then a diagnosis can be made and the diet altered accordingly.

Food Supplements Holistic physicians have become increasingly interested in the therapeutic uses of such food supplements as vitamins, minerals, amino acids (the building blocks of proteins), and digestive enzymes. This interest has been stimulated by Roger Williams's work on biochemical individuality and by studies such as those of the Nobel Prize winner Linus Pauling on the therapeutic use of large doses of vitamin C to prevent colds, slow the growth of cancer, and increase the immune response.

This area is even more fraught with controversy than other aspects of nutrition. For every study of the therapeutic use of large doses of vitamins or food supplements, there are critics questioning the methodology or outcome. Some opponents say that the mechanism of action of supplements is unknown, or that if taken in excess supplements can be toxic. Holistic physicians reply that the same is true of many commonly accepted orthodox treatments.

Although the debate rages, holistic physicians have drawn on those studies that do indicate benefits to help them formulate treatment plans for their patients. For example, many physicians, influenced by Pauling, use large doses of vitamin C to stimulate the immune system and to prevent and treat colds and viral infections; vitamin A may also be used to improve immune functioning; B vitamins are prescribed for depression and anxiety; zinc for acne; and vitamin E, garlic, and fish oil to improve circulation and lower blood pressure.

EXERCISE

The United States has experienced a "fitness boom" during the 1980s. Millions of formerly sedentary adults are walking and jogging, swimming, lifting weights, skiing, playing racketball and tennis, and doing yoga and martial arts. All of these activities may contribute to improved heart and lung functioning, relieve stress, and improve one's self-image. Although some exercise is beneficial for everybody, no one exercise is right for everybody. Jogging may be useful and pleasurable for many people, but the suggestion that all patients should run certainly lacks open-mindedness and respect for individual uniqueness.

A good holistic physician will try to tailor exercise regimens to the specific psychological and physical needs of his or her patients. For example, an overweight, agitated, and aggressive teenage boy may be advised to take up a martial art such as kung fu or karate. This type of activity will not only increase fitness and contribute to weight loss and relaxation, but also provide a constructive, disciplined outlet for his anger. On the other hand, an anxious middle-aged woman with arthritis may want to experiment with hatha yoga postures. This Indian exercise will help her to increase the circulation in her joints and the flexibility of her muscles, both so vital in treating arthritis. It also may give her a sense of mastery over the body that she believes has been betraying her.

HABIT CONTROL

Tens of millions of people in the United States are addicted to drugs, both legal and illicit. Millions more are compulsive eaters who are in a sense addicted to food. Conventional medical therapies, including medication to reduce craving, individual psychotherapies, and lectures on moderation have proved of remarkably little use in breaking these stubborn habits. Holistic practitioners, on the other hand, have begun to formulate approaches that combine a number of different techniques, all of which stress the importance of individual responsibility.

To begin with, the holistic approach is nonexclusive. It is compatible with and often includes the powerful mutual support and spiritual encouragement that such confessional groups as Alco-

Martial arts and other forms of exercise have become enormously popular in the 1980s. Millions of people have begun kicking up their heels in an effort to be more healthy.

holics Anonymous (AA), Narcotics Anonymous (NA), and Over-eaters Anonymous (OA) offer. But it also recognizes and deals with biological and behavioral factors that these groups do not address. A holistic physician has a number of techniques at his disposal. Acupuncture acts by some as yet unknown mechanism to reduce cravings of all kinds. Massage aids in relieving the muscular tension that accompanies withdrawal from alcohol, drugs, nicotine, or food. Exercise helps reduce weight, decrease anxiety, improve mood, and raise self-confidence. Dietary mod-ifications may diminish the biological craving for such sub-stances as alcohol and nicotine. Hypnosis can suggest reasons for giving up the addiction and support strategies to make it possible. Biofeedback and relaxation therapies can be employed to decrease, in a natural healthy way, the stress that addicts have been trying to relieve through alcohol, drugs, and food. Behavior modification therapies help people find alternative ways of cop-ing with stressful situations. The many options available in a holistic practice allow the program for each person to be tailored to meet his or her specific needs.

•   •   •   •

CHAPTER 5
. . . .
COMPLEMENTARY AND HOLISTIC MEDICINE

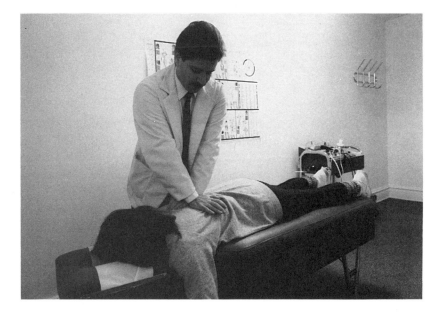

As we have seen, holistic medicine includes a variety of therapeutic approaches that lie outside the domain of conventional modern Western medicine. Some of these, such as the use of herbs and massage, are very much a part of our tradition but had until recently fallen into a state of disrespect, disregard, or disfavor. Some, such as psychic healing and homeopathy, have been part of a health underground in the United States and Western Europe, as well as in the Orient and South America. Still others, such as acupuncture, are products of other cultures and other ways of approaching health.

These approaches have sometimes been described as "alternative" medicines or disparaged as "fringe medicine" or "quackery." It is more accurate and more helpful to think of these methods—as the British do—as "complementary" to orthodox Western medicine. Some of the techniques, such as acupuncture and manipulation, for example, are practiced by physicians themselves or by nonphysician specialists. Others, such as massage, are generally administered by nonphysicians who have been specifically trained in that discipline. All of these techniques may be integrated into the practice of holistic medicine.

Massage, Osteopathy, and Chiropractic Massage

Massage is the systematic manipulation of the body's soft tissues, most particularly of the muscles and of the flesh that lies on top of them, but also of the joints. It is one of the oldest healing arts and one of the most widely used. Massage was used in China and India 5,000 years ago. And the Greek physician Hippocrates, writing in 430 B.C., noted the desirability of "rubbing the shoulder gently and smoothly" following its treatment for dislocation.

Most of the therapeutic massage that is practiced in the United States and Europe is a form of Swedish massage. This form of therapy, which includes a variety of different ways of rubbing, shaking, and kneading the skin and muscles, is used to relieve the muscle spasms and tightness that accompany acute injury and physical exertion. It also may help to increase circulation to joints that have become stiff from injury or arthritis. In recent years massage, which has the unusual quality of being both relaxing and energizing, has been used more and more commonly as a general stress-reduction technique for people who do not suffer from any particular illness. In addition to Swedish massage, there are a number of specialized forms. These include Chinese "acupressure" and Japanese "shiatzu," both of which stimulate the points of the body that are needled in acupuncture. Rolfing (named for its originator, the biochemist Ida Rolf), is another form of massage in which the "rolfer" tries to break up the adhesions between muscles and the connective tissue that envelops them. This process is said to allow muscles to function more smoothly and to permit the patient to stand and move in a more natural and relaxed way.

Manipulation, like massage, has been a significant part of most of the world's healing traditions, including those of ancient Egypt, China, and India. The two best-known modern therapies are osteopathy and chiropractic. Both are concerned with the manipulation of the bones, the joints, and most particularly the vertebrae, the bones that make up the spinal column.

Osteopathy Osteopathy (literally, "bone disease") was the creation of Andrew Taylor Still (1820–1917), who was trained as an orthodox physician but became disillusioned with the toxic side effects of many of the drugs he prescribed. Still discovered that if he put pressure on certain joints he could create a clicking sound that indicated, he felt, that he had properly repositioned bones that were misaligned. Still came to believe that this repositioning not only remedied such joint problems as bad backs and stiff necks, but also increased the local functioning of both the circulatory and the nervous systems. Because the nervous and circulatory systems supply the body's internal organs, Still concluded that osteopathic manipulation had enabled him to cure such conditions as pneumonia and infant diarrhea.

Andrew Taylor Still, the founder of osteopathy, was trained as an orthodox physician but went on to treat spinal, circulatory, and neurological conditions by repositioning bones that were misaligned.

A deaf boy receives acupuncture treatment in a Shanghai, China, school. Acupuncture is an important part of the Chinese system of healing, which also includes massage, manipulation, herbal remedies, and meditation.

Chiropractic The origins of chiropractic, from the Greek words *cheir* ("hand") and *praktikos* ("done by") were contemporary with those of osteopathy. In 1885 Daniel David Palmer, a Canadian nonphysician, performed manipulation on the neck of Harvey Lillard, a janitor in his building. After the manipulation Lillard, who had reportedly been deaf for 17 years, was able to hear. Palmer concluded that a "subluxation" (a partial dislocation of the vertebrae) in the neck had prevented the nerves that emerged from the spinal cord from transmitting the impulses necessary for proper hearing. He soon elaborated this belief into a system that closely resembled Still's: Subluxation of the spinal vertebrae was responsible, he believed, not only for local pain and discomfort, but also for dysfunction of internal organs.

Both Still and Palmer established colleges to teach their techniques and certify their practitioners. Originally, both osteopaths and chiropractors were quite separate from the medical profession. But in recent years osteopaths (D.O.s), who receive the same training as medical doctors (M.D.s) and are licensed to prescribe drugs and perform surgery, have come increasingly to resemble orthodox M.D.s in their practice. Few of them currently rely on the manipulative techniques that Still believed to be the essence of his work. In some states—California is one—the osteopath can legally change his title from Doctor of Osteopathy (D.O.) to Doctor of Medicine (M.D.).

Chiropractors (D.C.s), by contrast, have retained their emphasis on manipulation and remain outside the boundaries of mainstream medicine. Indeed, most orthodox physicians condemn their theories as simplistic and their training (only two years of college are required before 4 years of professional school, in which anatomy, physiology, nutrition, and relaxation therapies as well as manipulation are taught) as inadequate. The subluxations that chiropractors claim to be able to see in X rays and feel with their hands are, according to these critics, invisible and illusory. But in spite of this opposition, chiropractors are a major force in health care in the United States. As many as 8 million Americans visit an estimated 25,000 chiropractors each year.

Most holistic physicians—and many who are more conservative—are impressed with the effectiveness of spinal manipulation in treating some headaches and many cases of back pain. They are far less optimistic about the use of manipulation to treat acute and chronic internal illness.

Acupuncture

Acupuncture is an important part of the 5,000-year-old Chinese system of healing, which includes massage, manipulation, exercise, herbal remedies, and meditation. The ancient Chinese believed that human beings are a microcosm, a miniature version of the universe. Both man and the universe are subject to the natural laws of Tao, or "the way." The Chinese believed that when humans deviate from the way, the resulting disharmony might produce a disease. Chinese medicine in all its forms was concerned with helping people reestablish or preserve harmony, to follow the Tao. Interestingly, the most revered physicians in China were the philosophers, the ones who taught the way and thereby prevented illness from occuring.

According to the Chinese both the universe and humans have a male and female aspect, which they called yang and yin. The Chinese described yang as positive, active, hard, light, and hot, and associated it with the sun, the sky, and the day. Yin was viewed as negative, passive, soft, dark, cold, and connected to the moon, earth, and nighttime. Yin and yang were described as polarities that were constantly changing into one another, just as day becomes night and night becomes day.

The Chinese also believed that there are 12 organs in the body, all of which are either yin or yang. Generally speaking the more solid organs, such as the lungs, liver, and kidneys, were associated with yin; the hollow organs, such as the large intestine, gall bladder, and urinary bladder, with yang. The Chinese concept of these organs was not equivalent to the Western view. They believed that each organ has psychological qualities as well as a physical reality and was associated with particular tastes, smells and colors, seasons, and aspects of nature.

The Chinese believed that energy, which they called *chi*, flows from one organ to another during the course of each day. This energy was thought to travel in pathways called *meridians*, which connected the organs. It was discovered that during part of its length each meridian comes near the surface of the body, and that on each meridian there are points of particularly strong activity. Acupuncturists learned to stimulate these points with pressure from their fingers (acupressure), with metal or bone needles inserted to a depth ranging from one or two millimeters to one or two inches (acupuncture), and with heated herbs, which were applied directly to the skin or attached to the needles (moxibustion).

Nobody knows how the Chinese originally discovered these points or mapped out the meridians on which they lay. One legend has it that some warriors who had been injured by arrows and spears had unexpected improvements of chronic physical problems. The Chinese physicians observed the connections between the points of injury by these sharp instruments and the internal organs that were improved, and then asked a number of wise men to meditate on these connections. The result of their meditation was the map of the 14 major meridians and the more than 360 major acupuncture points that are still used today.

This story may well be a fable, but the acupuncture points are very real. They occur at areas of decreased electrical resistance

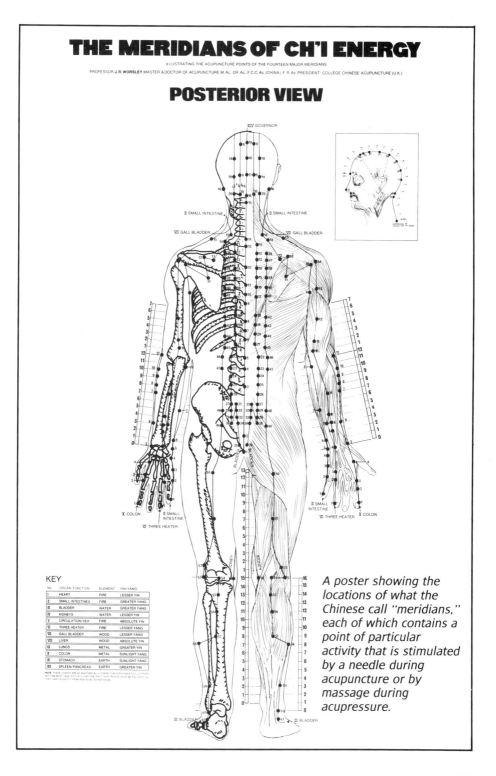

A poster showing the locations of what the Chinese call "meridians," each of which contains a point of particular activity that is stimulated by a needle during acupuncture or by massage during acupressure.

on the skin that can easily be located with modern instruments. Stimulation of these points will yield results that are quite compatible with the Chinese theory of their functions: For example, stimulation of the point called "Large Intestine 11" will regularly be helpful in relieving constipation and needling of "Stomach 36" will help with digestive problems and nausea.

Chinese physicians are not just concerned with using specific points to treat isolated symptoms. Their approach—holistic in every way—is to needle the combination of points that will balance the chi in the entire body and thereby balance both physical and emotional functions.

In order to determine which points are to be needled, the Chinese physician first studies the nature and symptoms of the illness and interviews the patient about possible causes. Then, because the Chinese physician believes that each part of the body is a microcosm of the whole, he or she looks for diagnostic information in these parts the way a Western doctor might examine the chemical composition of the blood or urine. The Chinese physician will study the form, shape, and coloring of the face and tongue, pay attention to the patient's voice and odor, and will feel the pulse of the radial artery on the thumb side of each wrist.

The pulse may be the most important single element in this type of diagnosis. The Chinese physician can feel six pulses at

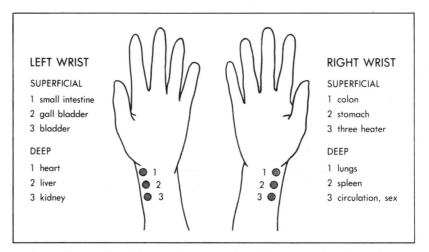

LEFT WRIST

SUPERFICIAL

1 small intestine
2 gall bladder
3 bladder

DEEP

1 heart
2 liver
3 kidney

RIGHT WRIST

SUPERFICIAL

1 colon
2 stomach
3 three heater

DEEP

1 lungs
2 spleen
3 circulation, sex

According to the Chinese, there are six pulses on each wrist—three superficial and three deep. The status and quality of each of these pulses correspond to those of specific internal organs.

each wrist—three close to the surface and three deeper—and believes that each of them corresponds to an internal organ (and to its corresponding meridian). The quality of each of these 12 pulses—its size, shape, and texture—indicates the status of the organ to which it corresponds. The pattern of the pulses provides a picture of the person's overall state of well-being. The lung pulse, for example, is the deep pulse at the most distal (closest to the fingers) place on the radial artery of the right hand. In the case of chronic pulmonary disease, the lung pulse may be soft, thready, and difficult to detect.

Once the physician has made the assessment, he or she selects the acupuncture points and puts in the needles, a process that is usually only slightly uncomfortable. The selections form a distinctive pattern designed to meet the unique present needs of this particular patient. In general, the acupuncturist is trying to increase "chi" energy where it is deficient and decrease it where it is excessive. When the treatment is over, there are palpable changes in the pulses that reflect changes in the organs and the state of the whole person—a return toward harmony and the Tao.

The task of understanding in Western scientific terms why acupuncture works has just begun. However, some research findings have already been made. Among them are the following:

- When a variety of different acupuncture points are needled, endorphins (natural morphinelike substances) are released in the brain; these produce a feeling of general well-being and relaxation.

- Acupuncture can be successfully used to create analgesia (lack of pain). This property makes it very useful for the treatment of chronic pain and as an alternative to general anesthesia in some surgical and dental operations.

- Acupuncture can increase local circulation in the area in which the needles have been placed. This increase in circulation is partly responsible for the effectiveness of acupuncture in treating arthritis and injuries such as sprains and tendonitis.

- Needling specific acupuncture points can produce a number of measurable physical changes including increases in the numbers of red and white blood cells, improved lung functioning, and a greater immune response.

Herbalism

The medicinal use of plants and herbs is as old as healing itself. For thousands of years herbs have been eaten fresh or dried, made into teas for internal consumption, and concocted into poultices, lotions, and oils to be rubbed on the skin.

Every society has discovered plants or herbs occurring in its territory that can be used to relieve pain, induce sleep, protect against infections, and reduce the swelling of sprains. Indeed until the beginning of the 19th century the vast majority of medicines were herbal medicines. Then, in 1803, the German pharmacist Frederick Serteurner isolated morphine, a powerful pain reliever, from the crude opium that was produced from poppies. From that time on, chemists in Europe and the United States have subjected thousands of plants to a detailed analysis so that they could extract the "active" ingredients from them. These substances were more potent (stronger in the same amounts), acted faster in the body, and were easier to measure and standardize than the herbs themselves.

Over the next 50 years thousands of drugs were isolated and synthesized from plants. Even now, if antibiotics grown on molds are included, the majority of all drugs still come from herbs. The herbs themselves, however, have lost their primary importance.

By the late 1960s herbalism was largely a historical curiosity. Physicians prescribed quinine for malaria, but knew nothing about the cinchona bark from which it was derived. And virtually everyone used synthetic acetylsalicylic acid (aspirin) to reduce pain but no one any longer chewed the willow bark that was the original source of its active ingredient.

Since the 1970s, however, there has been a significant revival of herbalism. This is in part a reaction against the side effects of potent pharmaceutical agents and in part a philosophical statement. People who are interested in the virtues of whole foods and integral, holistic methods of healing are predisposed to use whole plants as therapeutic agents rather than the substances that are isolated from them or the drugs that are synthesized to resemble them.

Moreover, herbalism is a consumer-oriented practice. Herbs can be grown in one's garden or purchased at health food stores. There are reference books available that explain which herbs are to be used for what ailment and how they should be prepared.

A medieval illustration of an herb garden. Plants and herbs have been used for their medicinal properties for thousands of years.

For example, an upset stomach may call for chamomile or ginger tea, whereas a combination of, uva ursi, parsley, corn silk, buchu, and juniper berries could be used to relieve swelling of the legs. No doctor's prescriptions are required.

This consumer orientation and philosophical predisposition are reinforced by the knowledge that whole plants contain many active ingredients other than the one usually extracted as a drug. Belief in herbalism is also bolstered by the conviction, based on some experience, that some of these other ingredients offset the side effects that come from the principal "active ingredient." The possibilities of dangerous side effects are further reduced because herbal prescriptions often contain several distinct substances, each of which is taken in very small doses.

Herbalists concede the virtues of drugs as lifesaving remedies when high dosage and rapid absorption are needed, but they claim that herbs, although not free of side effects, are both safer and more effective for the treatment of most chronic illnesses, for which medications usually have to be taken over a long period of time.

Homeopathy

Homeopathy (from the Greek *homios*, "like," and *pathos*, "suffering") is the creation of the distinguished German physician Samuel Hahnemann (1755–1845). Hahnemann formulated three basic laws for homeopathy: "like cures like"; the smaller the dose the more powerful the remedy ("the law of the minimal dose"); only one remedy is appropriate for each person at a given time ("the law of the single remedy"). All three of these laws defy accepted medical practice and even common sense, and yet homeopathy holds a strong appeal for many holistically oriented physicians and patients and, in a number of cases, seems to work.

Hahnemann discovered homeopathy in the course of trying to explain why cinchona bark was effective in the treatment of malaria. At the time, orthodox medicine had suggested that the "bitterness" of the bark accounted for its usefulness. Hahnemann, a skeptic and a critic of many of the medical practices of his day, decided to take daily doses of the bark to see what its effects might be. He first became "cold," then "languid and drowsy." His heart "began to palpitate." Later he experienced "unbelievable anxiety, trembling . . . rigidity of the limbs." He recognized that

The German physician Samuel Hahnemann first developed homeopathy, a medical philosophy that is popular among many holistic physicians.

these were the symptoms of malaria, the disease for which cinchona was the cure.

He then hypothesized that cinchona was curative *because* its ingestion created the symptoms that were characteristic of the disease. From this he concluded that "like cures like," or, more completely, that a substance that can produce certain symptoms in a healthy person can relieve the illness of someone who suffers from these symptoms.

Over the next 50 years Hahnemann went on to duplicate his cinchona experiment with some 90 other plant, animal, and mineral substances. He called these tests "provings" and the set of symptoms each substance produced, "drug pictures."

Hahnemann's first law was logically indefensible but it had been formulated in the past. It was known to the Greeks ("Through the like," Hippocrates had written, "disease is produced and through the application of the like it is cured") and to the 16th-century German physician Paracelsus. Hahneman's second law, "the law of the minimal dose," was even stranger. He maintained that the power of the remedy to relieve symptoms increased with increasing dilutions. If, for example, the appropriate symptom picture did not respond to a dilution of 1 part cinchona in 10, one ought to try a 1:100 or a 1:1,000 dilution.

According to Hahnemann's third law, that of the "single remedy," there is one and only one proper remedy for each symptom picture. In order to find this remedy the homeopathic physician must ask the patient dozens of detailed questions that orthodox physicians believe to be of little or no consequence. If he has an earache, which ear is it in? Is the eardrum pale or red? Does the pain increase with movement? Is it better with heat or cold? At night or during the day? Is he angry or tearful? Is his voice soft or loud? Once the homeopathic practitioner has constructed a symptom picture, he turns to the *Materia Medica*, which contains Hahnemann's provings and many hundreds more done by his successors, and selects the remedy whose picture most closely approximates the patient's.

From Hahnemann's time on, homeopathic remedies were prepared in a prescribed manner. One part of the substance—there are now more than 2,000 animal, plant, and mineral substances in use—was diluted with 9 parts of distilled water and alcohol. This mixture was shaken or "succussed" at least 40 times. This process of dilution might be continued indefinitely. The first di-

According to Hahnemann's homeopathic theory, the bark of the cinchona tree is an effective treatment for malaria because it produces in a healthy person symptoms similar to those of the disease.

lution is $1 \times x$, the second $2 \times x$ and so on up to 1,000,000x. Ultimately the diluted remedy is combined with another substance, usually milk sugar, and fashioned into tiny pills that melt on the tongue. Lower dilutions are given frequently for acute illnesses, higher ones less often for chronic problems.

During the 19th century homeopathy was in constant conflict with orthodox medicine. Hahnemann disparaged orthodox physicians as "allopathic" ("other than the disease") practitioners to indicate their tendency to prescribe remedies that bore no relation to the illness they were supposed to treat. The allopaths attacked the homeopaths, who often had orthodox allopathic training, as unscientific renegades. When homeopaths reported good results in treating cholera during the epidemics of the 1840s, allopaths refused to believe them. Still, in 1900 there were 22 homeopathic medical colleges and 14,000 or 15,000 homeopathic physicians in the United States—one-sixth to one-seventh of the nation's total number of doctors.

From 1900 to 1970 homeopathy remained strong in France, Germany, India, and in Latin America, as well as in Great Britain, where homeopaths are currently the physicians to the royal family. In the United States, however, the decline of homeopathy was rapid. Reforms within allopathic medicine, the therapeutic potency of many drugs that were isolated from plants, and continued political opposition and harassment all but obliterated homeopathy from medical practice.

In the 1970s this situation began to change. To a new generation of physicians and patients, homeopathy began to look interesting again. It was holistic in the sense that it took into account a vast array of psychological, physical, and social symptoms and prescribed according to the unique picture of each person. Its remedies, given in tiny doses, were free from the side effects of conventional drugs. It was thought to work in a more natural way, by strengthening the body's natural healing forces rather than by attacking the disease. And it was democratic: The principles of diagnosis and prescription could be learned and practiced by nonphysicians as well as physicians. Finally, homeopathy seemed to be effective in some cases where all orthodox remedies had failed.

How and why homeopathy works is a mystery. Some proponents compare its effectiveness to the use of vaccines to produce immunity. Some vaccines, such as those used for polio and measles, are tiny doses of the substances that in large doses produce the disease. Perhaps, the theory runs, homeopathic remedies create a similar kind of immunity in those who receive them. Others point to a drug such as Ritalin, which in a normal person produces profound stimulation but in a hyperactive child produces calm: Here is an example of "like cures like."

Neither of these explanations is entirely satisfactory, and neither explains how a homeopathic remedy that is so diluted that *no* molecules of the substance remain in the sugar in which it

The shrine at Lourdes, France, where many people claim to have witnessed miraculous psychic healings of seemingly incurable illnesses.

has been mixed can possibly work. Homeopaths speak of the "vibration" of the substance being transmitted or of a profound change in the molecular structure of the sugar in the pill, but neither has been demonstrated.

Some people suggest that homeopathy works because patients expect that it will work. The clinical experience of many holistic physicians runs counter to this explanation. Most homeopaths agree that homeopathy is particularly effective in infants and in animals, who are of course less likely to be influenced by positive expectations.

At any rate, thousands of physicians in the United States are convinced that homeopathy can be therapeutic, and scientific studies are beginning to appear that confirm these convictions. Extremely dilute homeopathic preparations have proven effective in altering chemical reactions. And one clinical study, showing the effectiveness of homeopathic remedies in treating rheumatoid arthritis, was published in 1980 in the prestigious *British Journal of Pharmacology*.

Psychic Healing

Psychic healing refers to those kinds of physical healings that cannot be explained in biological, medical, or psychological terms. These include sudden improvement following prayer, changes brought about by other people (medicine men, priests, and so on), by groups (as in group prayer), or by the patient's presence in a sacred place. Psychic healing is also reported to occur in places such as the shrine at Lourdes, France, where during the 1850s Bernadette Soubirous had visions of the Virgin Mary and where hundreds have subsequently described "miracle cures." Prayer and positive thinking, laying on of hands, and religious rituals are some of the ways people try to bring about psychic healing.

Numerous examples of psychic healing are recorded in the Old and New Testaments, the best known being the cures attributed to Jesus. In the biblical instances, as well as in many modern examples, psychic healing seems to have two therapeutic components. The first is related to the hopeful expectation and the faith of the person seeking help. The second is connected to the healing power of the helper.

The former aspect of psychic healing relates to what medicine has long described as the *placebo* ("I please," in Latin) response. A placebo is generally a pharmacologically inactive substance given by a physician to a patient who wants, but in the physician's estimate does not need, medication. Because patients invest these placebos with the hope of relief, they often do act as therapeutic agents. Still, medicine paid little attention to placebos, using them mostly as controls to which the activity of "real drugs" was compared.

The second major kind of psychic healing depends for its efficacy on some special power that resides in the healer. This healing force, of which orthodox medicine continues to be extremely skeptical, does appear to be supported by some interesting evidence. In the 1960s the Canadian biochemist Bernard Grad studied the effects of a healer's hands on sprouting barley seeds. He divided the seeds into three groups and treated the water with which they were irrigated in the following ways: The water used in the first control group came from the tap; the second control group was irrigated with water that had been put in flasks and held by people who had no stake in the outcome of the experiment; the third sample was irrigated from water in flasks that had been held by a well-known healer named Estebany.

The results were striking. The seeds that had been irrigated by the water that Estebany held sprouted earlier than the others. After five days they were significantly taller and richer in chlorophyll.

In the early 1970s, Dr. Dolores Krieger, a professor of nursing, became interested in this work. Within a few years Krieger had begun a series of studies on the effect of healers on humans. She found that when a healer repeatedly put his or her hands on or near a patient, the patient's level of hemoglobin—a vital constituent of red blood cells—increased significantly. Krieger believed that an increase in hemoglobin reflected an overall improvement in health and well-being and indicated that the healer was communicating some as yet immeasurable physical force that produced this change.

Because she was a clinician and teacher as well as a researcher, Krieger wanted to see if people who were not defined as specially gifted healers could be taught to produce the same results. She repeated her study, this time with groups of nurses working on hospital wards. The results, as published in the *American Journal of Nursing*, showed that nurses who touched their patients with a "healing intention" produced significantly greater increases in hemoglobin in their patients than those who spent the same amount of time providing routine nursing care. Krieger concluded that this healing therapeutic technique, which she called "therapeutic touch," was a "natural human potential which could be done by any person who had a fairly healthy body, a strong intent to help or heal sick persons and the ability to project healing intentions to others."

At present holistic physicians are exploring other aspects of psychic healing. It is quite possible that these methods, with their emphasis on drug-free forms of self-help and mutual help, will become an increasingly popular option in the future.

•   •   •   •

CHAPTER 6

HOLISTIC MEDICINE IN PRACTICE

Each physician's approach to holistic medicine is different and so is his or her approach to each patient. This is essential if one is to treat people in a way that is comprehensive, flexible, and respectful of each person's uniqueness. The following chapter is a personal account of the methods I used in treating three young people with three different health problems. I have changed the names and some identifying details, but have tried to preserve some of the significant interactions and therapeutic strategies and the spirit of our work together. It should also be noted that holistic medicine remains a controversial approach. It is often tremendously effective, as these three case studies will attest, but, like orthodox medicine, it does not necessarily work for everyone.

Michael

I had met Michael in his parents' home before his mother called to ask me for an appointment. I remembered him as a small, thin, shy boy with sandy hair who looked younger than his 13 years. "He's got asthma and it's getting worse," his mother informed me. "He's taking pills and he uses an inhaler but he's still wheezing. His pediatrician doesn't know what to do with him." It sounded as if Michael's mother was herself desperate and out of breath.

"Does Michael want to come?" I asked her.

"I don't know. I think so."

I asked her to have him call me. I have discovered that it is far better for young people to make their own appointments with me. That way the patient will not decide to see me just to please his or her parents, or decide not to see me to rebel against them. The decision to come is theirs just as the responsibility for carrying out a therapeutic plan will be. A little while later Michael called to make his appointment.

I first saw Michael briefly with his mother and then asked her to leave the room. Two minutes after I closed the door, he became animated. When I had met him at his parents' house he always seemed to stare at his shoes or into the distance over my shoulder. Now he was looking right at me, almost begging me to understand what he was saying.

His asthma had bothered him on and off since he could remember, but it had gotten worse in recent months.

"Since when?"

"September," he said. And September turned out to be the beginning of a year in a new school, one where he knew few people and felt out of place. When I pressed him, he told me he was avoiding doing the work in math and English that he found difficult and that each week he seemed to be falling further behind. To make himself feel better he ate junk food and drank soft drinks, which he craved.

He had always had lots of colds and many sinus infections for which antibiotics had been prescribed. Just a few weeks ago he

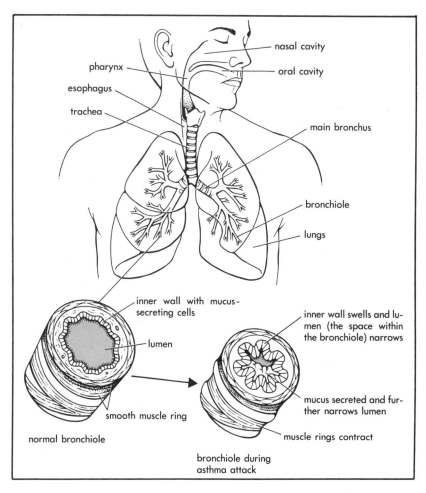

nasal cavity

pharynx

oral cavity

esophagus

trachea

main bronchus

bronchiole

lungs

inner wall with mucus-
secreting cells

inner wall swells and lu-
men (the space within
the bronchiole) narrows

lumen

mucus secreted and fur-
ther narrows lumen

smooth muscle ring

muscle rings contract

normal bronchiole

bronchiole during
asthma attack

A diagram of the respiratory system illustrates the physical changes that take place in the bronchioles during an asthma attack.

had had another sinus infection. When I asked Michael for more details, he told me that he had a "metallic taste" in his mouth, which, according to Chinese medicine, is a sign of dysfunction in either the lungs or large intestine.

When I examined Michael, I saw a thin, anxious boy whose ribs pushed against his skin. He had the barrellike chest that is characteristic of people who have to use all their muscles to force the air out of their lungs. I could hear the wheezes in his breathing and, when I touched his back, feel that some of the vertebrae in the middle of his spine were turned to one side.

The sugar and caffeine in many soft drinks can make a person more vulnerable to infection. Dr. Gordon advised an asthma patient to eliminate these beverages from his diet in order to ease his symptoms.

I did some adjustments on his spine to put the vertebrae back where they belonged, and then took his pulse. The lung pulse was low and so too was the spleen pulse. In Chinese medicine the spleen includes the pancreas, which itself has several functions including the metabolism of sugar. The spleen also regulates the immune system and "gives energy" to the lungs. So it was not surprising to me that Michael was craving sweets and having many infections, and that both of these were common symptoms among people with asthma. In the Chinese system sugar craving and a depleted immune system are connected with low spleen energy, and low spleen energy produces low lung energy.

After the spinal adjustment Michael seemed to stand a bit straighter, and after an acupuncture treatment his breathing was easier and he seemed to have more energy. The metal taste, he said, was gone.

When I spoke with Michael about his illness, I told him that the chronic condition had become a crisis because of his worry about school and the new school year. I explained that the antibiotics that were used to treat his colds and sinus problems had not really cured the basic weakness in his lungs or his spleen and may have, in the long run, made him vulnerable to other, more resistant bacteria. I explained that in Chinese medicine the lungs were associated with depression and anxiety. Being in a new school had increased his anxiety and decreased his lung energy. Because he was bright but was having trouble in school I also suggested, first to him and later to him and his mother, that he be tested for learning disabilities.

I also spoke with Michael and his mother about his diet. I pointed out that the sugar and caffeine in soft drinks would deplete his pancreas and immune system and make him even more vulnerable to fatigue and infection. I recommended that he stop drinking them. I also suggested that he remove wheat and milk, common allergy producers, from his diet and avoid junk food (which is filled with sugar), salt, and food additives.

When it became clear that this would mean that Michael would have to bring his own lunch to school, his mother became anxious. Then Michael began to get agitated. I pointed this out to them. Michael said that he too had noticed that whenever his mother got "uptight" he felt it in his own body.

"Forget about her anxiety," I said, and Michael laughed for the first time.

I asked Michael if he would be willing to bring his own food to school and he said he would. He was "very tired of being sick" and if changing his diet would help, he could do it.

"One more thing," I added. "Every morning when you wake up I want you to stand in front of a mirror with your shirt off, and pound your chest and shout like Tarzan for fifteen minutes." That, I explained, "will help stimulate your lungs." Michael looked at me as if I were crazy but said he would try.

Two weeks later Michael came back to see me. His color was better, he had put on a few pounds, and he had more energy. He was breathing easily now and told me that except for one or two "emergencies" he had stopped taking all his asthma medicine. The food that he took to school—which his mother had feared would set him apart from the other kids—actually brought him closer to them. The raw vegetables, fruits, and nuts made him an object of fascination. Several students who had chronic colds and allergies wondered if they should go on a similar diet, and most of them were amused by his stories of the strange doctor who stuck needles in him.

"What about the pounding on your chest?"

"Well," he confessed, "at first I felt like an imbecile, but after a while I got into it." The idea of a skinny little kid acting like Tarzan made him laugh, and somehow much of his fear and self-consciousness seemed to be going away. His mood had lifted. And the testing for learning disabilities? "Well," he confided, "it turns out I have them." He considered the tutor his parents had found to be "a pain," but he had to admit he was doing better in school and was far less anxious about it.

Michael came regularly once a month for four months and then decided that because his asthma attacks had all but disappeared and he was doing well in school, he would stop his regular visits. He was no longer pounding his chest, but he was getting good exercise playing soccer. He assured me he was continuing on the diet. Just before he left he asked if I would be there if he needed me. I said I would.

Laura

Laura was 18 when she first came to see me. I had treated her father and brother for back problems so she knew what to expect when she called: needles, a strange diet, maybe some weird advice. And she knew, even before I told her so, that she would have to do most of the work herself.

When she came into the office she told me that she had had terrible acne since her period began at age 14. She pointed to a dozen red blotches on her pretty, tanned face and informed me that the ones I would find on her chest and back were much worse. She was also overweight, and was finding it impossible to lose the 10 or 15 pounds she wanted to.

When I asked her if she was in school, she told me she had just finished her freshman year at college. She was trying to decide on a major now, and although she had never had problems with her studies, she found herself strangely shaken. She wanted to major in the performing arts, perhaps even become a professional dancer, but her father, an attorney, said it was "impractical and self-defeating"; she should study history or economics to prepare herself for law school or business school. She was "not that good a dancer," he added, unnecessarily and apparently inaccurately. Besides, she was far too heavy.

Laura did not particularly want to go to law school or business school, but she also said she did not want to disappoint her father. When I asked why that was so important, she told me that for different reasons he had been very disappointed in both her mother and brother. "Besides," she added, he always "seemed to be right" when he had given her advice before. He was, she assured me, "a very smart man." Laura was afraid that if she went against him now, she would suffer later. She told me she had spent most of the summer going over all this in her mind. Sometimes at the pool where she worked as a lifeguard, or in dance classes, someone would tell her she looked "spaced out." Then she realized she had been off in another world, debating the merits of dance versus law and business.

As I took a detailed physical history, I learned that for the past year Laura's periods had been brief and scanty. She had premenstrual syndrome (PMS) for a week before each one. During this time her stomach, breasts, hands, and feet were swollen. Even her face was puffy. Her joints were also stiff, and she was cranky and depressed. She moved her bowels only every three days. But even at other times during the month she was constipated. She knew that she should not be eating the junk food and sweets that she indulged in, but she did not feel as if she were "pigging out," so she could not understand why she kept gaining weight. She told me all this in a frustrated, angry tone of voice.

Sitting with Laura, hearing her dilemma at choosing a major, listening to her physical symptoms, the word "stuck" kept coming to my mind. "You're stuck," I finally blurted out. "You can't decide whether to major in what you or your father wants. Your body won't let go either: You can't move your bowels. You swell up like a balloon before your period and you never get rid of all that water. Weight stays on. Even your periods are stingy. It's no wonder you have the acne. It's your body's way of trying to get rid of substances that aren't coming out in your urine or stools."

I do not know what I expected from Laura—maybe an argument or maybe a quizzical look. But to my amazement she simply said, "I know," and then, "So what do I do?"

I put Laura on a fast of 10 to 12 pounds of watermelon a day for 7 days and 3 quarts of spring water a day. Watermelon, I

Dr. Gordon treated an unhappy young woman for a variety of physical and emotional problems. Realizing that she was serious about a career in dance, he urged her to pursue it even though her father disapproved.

explained, has been used in the Middle East for thousands of years by herbalists. They discovered by trial and error that it was a natural diuretic, a water remover. Fasting on watermelons would give her body a rest, help her kidneys eliminate the extra fluid that her body was retaining. And yes, she was healthy enough to do this fast, as long as she did it under my close supervision.

Following this she was to eat only raw food for 14 days, then a diet comprising 70% raw food and 30% cooked food. No sugar, no processed or junk food. Every day she was to drink two to three quarts of spring water. The two weeks of raw food would provide plenty of bulk for her bowels and would help her lose weight. She would get protein from raw eggs and from shellfish such as shrimp and scallops marinated in lemon juice. The water would stimulate both her kidneys and her intestinal functioning.

Then I told Laura that she would have to get unstuck psychologically as well as physically. I suggested that her weight problem and her acne were psychological as well as physical problems. She got what psychiatrists call a "secondary gain" from these apparently troublesome symptoms. If she was 15 pounds overweight she could not possibly dance professionally. If she had bad skin, she would become so self-conscious that she would avoid performing. She was saying she wanted to dance, but her symptoms were keeping her loyal to her father—and stuck.

"You have to know," I told her, "not just intellectually, but instinctively, that you can't choose your life's work just to please your father." I suggested that when she went back to school she might want to talk to a psychotherapist about all this. "For now, however, I want you every day to put on some fast music and dance like a madwoman, in front of a mirror."

Sometimes people protest when I give them this kind of assignment. They do not have the time, they say; the music will bother others; they feel ridiculous. But Laura just listened as I explained that dancing and sweating would help open the pores in her skin and that the exercise would burn off calories as well. And dancing in front of a mirror would help her to lose her self-consciousness. Most of all, dancing wildly would be something Laura would enjoy.

A week later Laura came back eight pounds lighter and much happier. Much of the fluid had gone. Her skin was better and her face had lost its puffiness. There was now "no question" that she was going to major in dance. She "loved" the dancing in front of a mirror, she told me, grinning.

I saw Laura every week for six weeks during the summer. Now, a year and a half later, I still see her every couple of months when she comes home on vacation. Within six weeks her bowels had become regular, her PMS and swelling negligible, and her skin, though not flawless, much clearer. When she went back to school she saw a psychotherapist once a week for a year. The therapist helped her to see that she did not have to make up for her father's disappointment with her mother and brother. She has kept off the 15 pounds and is now dancing with the university's best company. When her father frets about her future, she tells him that if she does not become a professional dancer, she will probably earn her living as a dance therapist—working with young people who are as stuck as she once was.

Steven

Steven was 14 when his mother asked him to call me. A charming, handsome black young man who was the youngest of five children—and the only one who had managed to stay out of trouble—he was his mother's and his grandmother's "darling."

He also had an ulcer in his stomach and periodically suffered from terrifying anxiety attacks.

The first anxiety attack had come two years before, after he and one of his older brothers had smoked some marijuana. They were horsing around in the house and then his brother left to be with friends. Steven, who had been giggling and wrestling just a few minutes before, suddenly felt sweaty and cold. His heart was pounding so hard he thought it would break his ribs. Gasping for breath, he was sure he was going to die.

The next attack came three months later, but after that they increased in frequency. Meanwhile, Steven began to have stomach pains. They were worst in the morning, but sometimes they came on in the middle of the day. He went to his pediatrician, who took X rays and discovered the beginnings of an ulcer. He prescribed medications to suppress acid secretions, a bland diet, and tranquilizers. The medication made Steven nauseous and the bland diet did not help. The tranquilizers took the edge off the anxiety attacks, but they did not do anything to stop them, and they made him so sleepy that he would nod off in class.

In my first conversation with Steven it was hard to sort out exactly what was causing his anxiety attacks. Sometimes marijuana would cause one, but other times he would have an attack after not having smoked in weeks. He thought school was somewhat boring, but he was fairly well liked by his classmates. Home was "okay." His mother was a little too protective, his grandmother "pretty old-fashioned," and one of his brothers, a bully who drank and smoked too much, was threatening, but Steven was "used to it" and "loved them all."

At first Steven and I set to work on his physical problems. I told him to stop the medications and the bland diet, which was loaded with milk products, to which it turned out Steven was allergic. In fact it seemed that the diet that was supposed to help was actually making his stomach worse.

In place of his previous regime, I put him on raw cabbage juice and raw potato juice on an empty stomach in the morning and, for the rest of the day, a diet that was mostly brown rice, vegetables, and fish. I eliminated milk and milk products totally. The cabbage and potato juice remedy, which I had learned from an Indian herbalist, seemed very strange to Steven and his mother. But his grandmother, a Mississippi woman who had lived in the country, had once used a similar remedy. The rest of the diet caused some problems at first because Steven's mother was not keen on making a separate meal for him. But when Steven decided to take over his own cooking, things calmed down.

Then we tried to uncover the cause of Steven's anxiety attacks and went to work on helping him deal with the symptoms. At each weekly meeting I treated Steven with acupuncture. Initially he was terrified of the needles, but he let me put them in when I said they would relax him. Halfway through the first treatment he was smiling. By the end of it, he was claiming that it was "better than grass."

I took this opportunity to suggest that Steven stop smoking marijuana. Even if it was not the cause of the anxiety attacks, smoking seemed to remind him of his first attack. Perhaps it created a "flashback"; at any rate, it made him afraid he was going to have another. Besides, acupuncture was more relaxing. He agreed that continuing to smoke did not make much sense.

Next I taught Steven how to relax on his own. I used progressive muscular relaxation first, and then a guided imagery exercise to help him to warm his fingers. I made an audiotape of both parts for him and encouraged him to practice daily at home.

Many teenagers—and younger children as well—tend to be very good at these exercises, and Steven, who was quite imaginative, was no exception. Within a week he was able to relax quickly and increase the temperature in his fingers by several degrees. Now when the anxiety attacks came, even if his heart was pounding crazily, Steven would sit down and breathe slowly and deeply, tensing and untensing his muscles. Soon he would relax, his fingers would get warm, and he would feel his pulse grow more quiet and sure.

Our success in dealing with his ulcer and reducing the symptoms of his anxiety attacks created a bond of trust between Steven and myself. Within a couple of months, he was able to find what made him anxious and tell me about it: He felt too dependent on his mother and felt unable to leave the restrictive circle of her concern. Some anxiety attacks, he discovered, were triggered by her absence, or simply by being alone in her house or in a threatening situation—a difficult test coming up, a possible fight on the street— where she could not help.

But as we soon learned, the worst attacks would come when Steven was unable to contact his father, who had left the house six years before, and periodically disappeared completely for days.

As we sifted through the events surrounding these attacks, Steven discovered that fears for his father's safety and dreams of his death had preceded the attacks. These in turn created fears for his own safety.

It took us perhaps six months to get to this point. We then decided to work with the family situation that was so clearly contributing to Steven's anxiety. From time to time we asked his mother and grandmother to come to our sessions so that he and I could both talk to them. We would discuss the importance of their giving Steven more freedom and treating him as if he were capable of caring for himself—in short, of letting him go. They became aware of their fears for Steven, their own need to keep their "baby" close to home. It was, we concluded, based not so much on a realistic concern for Steven as on *their* anxiety about being without him. Soon his mother and grandmother felt more comfortable allowing Steven to spend more time with his friends, to have later curfews.   Next Steven and I met with Steven's father. Joint meetings with Steven's mother and father—who continued, six years after their divorce—to use every one of Steven's symptoms as an occasion to insult each other—had turned out not to be useful. Steven told his father how distressing his long and unpredictable periods of absence were. Once his father realized this he agreed to spend more time with Steven when he came into town, and to stay in contact when he was away. This consistency allowed Steven to feel less threatened by his father's absence and, as time went on, less dependent on him.

Over the next six months the anxiety attacks diminished in frequency and severity. When one occurred, Steven was now able both to regulate it and to explore its causes on his own: He was becoming more independent of his parents as well as of me. A year after I first saw him, Steven went to sleep-away camp for the first time in his life. Two-thirds of the way through the summer he wrote me a card: "NO ANXIETY ATTACKS!!!"

•   •   •   •

CHAPTER 7

· · · · · · · · · · · · · ·

THE FUTURE OF HOLISTIC MEDICINE

The practice of holistic medicine has grown at a phenomenal rate since the 1970s, when the first holistic physicians began trying new approaches. Some of these pioneer doctors pooled their resources and opened the first holistic health centers. These institutions have become more and more widespread as holistic medicine has expanded. This chapter will sketch the development of holistic health centers and will then highlight the way holistic medicine is being incorporated into mainstream practice. It will conclude with an examination of the ways in which holistic medicine may help shape the future of health care in the United States.

HOLISTIC HEALTH CENTERS

In the early 1970s Dr. Norman Shealy, a neurosurgeon who had become disillusioned with the reasons for and the results of many neurosurgical procedures, began to combine behavior modification and relaxation therapies with nonsurgical pain-reduction techniques to treat people with chronic back pain—people on whom he would previously have operated.

Soon Shealy and others were enlarging their practices, increasing the kinds of treatments they used, and creating the first holistic health centers. Shealy now directs the Pain and Health Rehabilitation Center in Springfield, Missouri, which combines relaxation therapies, physical fitness, altered diet, hypnosis, biofeedback, and psychotherapy with conventional medical therapies to treat a whole range of chronic illness.

At Shealy's center and elsewhere physicians work in collaboration with nurse practitioners, psychologists, social workers, acupuncturists, chiropractors, homeopaths, and faith healers. Some of the centers, such as Shealy's, are residential. Patients

In the early 1970s the neurosurgeon Dr. Norman Shealy founded one of the first holistic health centers.

can come for one or more weeks to live in a retreat setting and learn techniques to help themselves. They then return home to use what they have learned, always maintaining the option of returning to the center for "refresher courses" in the future.

Other centers, like Drs. Carl and Stephanie Simonton's Center for Cancer Counseling and Rehabilitation in Fort Worth, Texas, were formed to deal with specific conditions. Some, such as Dr. Walt Stoll's Holistic Health Center in Lexington, Kentucky, and the Wholistic Health and Nutrition Institute in Mill Valley, California, have always dealt with a wide variety of major and minor illnesses, and function as large holistic general practices for the surrounding community.

Some of these centers have had a distinctively spiritual emphasis. For example, the 11 Wholistic Health Centers that the Reverend Granger Westburg established in the 1970s and 1980s explicitly attempted to restore the Christian church's healing mission. Located in churches, they relied on a three-member team of physician, nurse practitioner, and pastoral counselor (a minister trained in counseling and psychotherapy) as primary caregivers. Others were more secular or eclectic, freely combining medical techniques with meditations borrowed from different cultures.

In 1978 Leslie Kaslof's Wholistic Dimensions of Healing noted approximately 50 holistic health centers in the United States. Five years later there were more than 200. Today there are even more. Although there is no association of holistic health centers comparable to the American Hospital Association, there is an American Holistic Medical Association (AHMA) to which the medical directors of virtually all these centers and many other holistic physicians belong. The AHMA, which was founded by Dr. Shealy in 1978, has more than 400 physician members. Through its national and local meetings, journal, and newsletter, it provides opportunities for holistic physicians to exchange ideas, a format for organizational activity, training programs, and a source of mutual support and encouragement.

Wellness Centers

The most obvious influence of holistic medicine has been on the creation of hospital-based and corporate wellness programs. Because these centers are concerned with promoting health rather

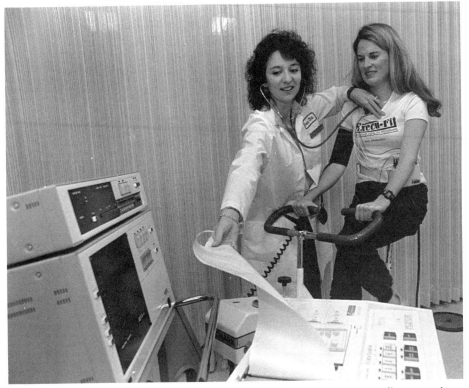

An increasing number of corporations are providing or recommending exercise and wellness programs for their employees.

than treating disease they were initially seen as an adjunct to the care provided by orthodox physicians. Over time, however, their perspective and practices have also begun to change the medical care provided by the hospitals and corporations.

One of the earliest of the wellness centers was the Swedish Wellness Center at the Swedish Medical Center in Englewood, Colorado. Modeled after John Travis's original wellness center in Mill Valley, California, it has subsequently become a model itself for hundreds of wellness centers in hospitals around the country.

Although these wellness programs vary, they generally begin with individual counseling sessions and detailed questionnaires that are designed to help participants see the relationship between their behavior and their health. The answers they provide are used as a basis for showing them that what and how much they drink, eat, smoke, and exercise, how they drive, the way they work, and how they get along with their families will affect the way they feel physically and emotionally.

For those who decide to participate, wellness centers offer courses in relaxation therapies, smoking cessation, aerobics, and yoga, as well as individual and group counseling. Because they are generally available to hospital personnel they serve to introduce the entire staff to a more holistic perspective. They are also economically advantageous to the hospital. They reduce absenteeism among staff and also seem to attract more paying clients than hospitals that do not offer these choices.

Economic considerations, as well as concern for the health of their employees, have also been of preeminent importance in the adoption of wellness programs by many corporations. The amount of money that corporations spend on health care—more than $150 billion per year—is enormous, and the loss in income and productivity from preventable illness is even larger. Corporate wellness programs often include meditation and relaxation therapies to relieve stress, yoga and aerobics, fitness programs, and individual and group counseling to reduce alcohol and substance abuse, as well as early screening for high blood pressure and cancer. One program, begun in 1985 by the University of California Medical School in San Franscico, involves some 14 major corporations, including Apple Computer, the Bank of America, Xerox, and Lockheed.

Holistic Medicine in the Medical School and Hospital

It is not easy to introduce change in hospitals and medical schools. If a department of psychiatry offers an hour-long lecture on relaxation therapies, then there is one hour less for other subjects. No department wants to give up its time and no expert wants to see his or her field shortchanged. And any attempt to bring about change must first be explored and approved by a long succession of committees.

Given these obstacles, and the critical light that a holistic perspective sheds on many current medical practices, it is remarkable to see the changes that are taking place in some hospitals and medical schools. At Harvard Medical School, for example, an entirely new way of approaching medical education called "The New Pathway" is in place. It attempts to integrate the various aspects of medical education and emphasizes respectful listening to patients and attention to the familial and social worlds in which they live.

At Beth Israel, one of Harvard's main teaching hospitals, there is a department of behavioral medicine directed by Dr. Herbert Benson, a heart specialist. Benson, who has written a popular book called *The Relaxation Response* as well as many academic papers, has tried for the last 15 years to bring the scientific method to the study of relaxation therapies and meditations. His original research involved the study of the beneficial effect of relaxation on blood pressure. Currently he and his staff are particularly concerned with positive changes in the immune system brought on by meditation.

If Harvard and its hospitals are leaders in creating a more holistic perspective, they are certainly not alone. Acupuncture and relaxation therapies are a major part of the treatment at the Lemuel Shattuck Hospital for Chronic Diseases in Boston. At UCLA Medical School, a comprehensive pain clinic combines relaxation, guided imagery, acupuncture, dietary modification, and individual and group psychotherapy in its program; UCLA's continuing medical education department also sponsors a well-attended program of acupuncture education for physicians. At Yale Medical School the pioneering work of Carl and Stephanie Matthews Simonton in using guided imagery to increase the immune response in cancer patients is now being subjected to intensive investigation. And at the University of South Carolina's School of Nursing a major study of Dolores Krieger's therapeutic touch is under way. In addition, professors in increasing numbers of medical schools have created elective courses in holistic medicine. The interest in holistic medical education is not confined to physicians who work in wellness programs or teach in medical schools. The accumulating medical evidence and the demands of patients, physicians' experiences in dealing with their own health problems, and the desire to be of help to others are all combining to goad doctors who would never call themselves holistic to look into some aspects of the holistic approach.

Doctors who 15 years ago scoffed at reports that inadequate nutrition might cause cancer have learned from studies at the National Cancer Institute that high-fat diets have been implicated in breast and bowel cancer and that high-fiber diets may help prevent these diseases. They are changing their own eating habits and advising their patients to do likewise. Although they themselves may not claim expertise in the area, many physicians are recommending that their patients attend exercise and stress-reduction programs. Some may still be puzzled by meditation, but are able to appreciate the technical impressiveness of biofeedback and are flexible enough to include it in their practice.

Physicians are now more likely to ask psychiatrists, psychologists, and psychiatric social workers to provide their patients with the individual attention necessary for dealing with the emotional aspects and familial consequences of catastrophic and chronic illness. Orthopedic surgeons may refer some patients with intractable back pain to the chiropractor for whom 10 years earlier they had nothing but contempt. Physicians who deal with chronic pain are feeling more comfortable about broadening their approach to include massage, hypnosis, and acupuncture. And many physicians are learning to listen more carefully to the concerns of those whom they are paid to help. They are also paying more attention to the latest research on diet, exercise, homeopathy, or acupuncture that their increasingly well-informed patients are bringing to them.

Dr. Herbert Benson conducts scientific tests on a Tibetan monk. Dr. Benson, a heart specialist, has done intensive studies on the beneficial effects of relaxation therapies and meditation.

THE FUTURE OF HOLISTIC MEDICINE

As a population we are living longer and are therefore more likely to develop the chronic diseases for which the holistic approach is most useful. And as a society we are unfortunately perpetuating the social and environmental conditions that make chronic disease more likely. For these reasons and more it seems likely that holistic medicine will play an ever-increasing role in the future, and will continue to transform the nature of medical education, research, and care.

Medical Education

To increasing numbers of medical students and young physicians the holistic perspective is more interesting, complex, rewarding, and emotionally satisfying than the somewhat more narrow orthodox approach. As the practice of holistic medicine becomes more widespread in the future it will attract even more bright and sensitive medical students.

Pressure from such students, and from the growing numbers of young faculty members who have been exposed in their formative years to holistic medicine, should increasingly influence the nature of medical education. Eventually it must broaden to include the healing traditions of other cultures—Chinese, Indian, Native American, and African, among others—as well as healing practices neglected in our own. It will deepen to include a greater understanding of the psychological causes and effects of illness. And it will become increasingly democratic, embracing a far greater variety of self-help techniques and a more collaborative way of thinking about the practice of medicine. Some experts predict that within the next 15 or 20 years most medical schools will offer comprehensive courses in nutrition and food allergies; well-designed and thorough electives in Chinese medicine and acupuncture; training in self-regulation therapies; and an introduction to manipulative therapies.

Medical Research

Already superbly trained young researchers are bringing their expertise to bear on the study of practices that are included in the holistic approach, including relaxation and meditation, vegetarian and macrobiotic diets, yoga, acupuncture, guided im-

James Harrell, deputy director of the U.S. Office of Health Promotion and Disease Prevention, takes a run around the Washington Mall. Medical practitioners of all persuasions advocate regular exercise as a means of reducing stress and attendant health problems.

agery, and homeopathy. As the number of these researchers grows, more and more studies will attempt to explain how and why these approaches work. Some will explore what chi energy is, how it functions in organs and how it relates to our own concepts of biochemistry and physiology. Others will map out the intermediate steps between the mental processes of guided imagery and the increase in functioning of the organs that are imaged. Moreover, I suspect that a new kind of research methodology will be developed, one that goes beyond statistical probability to attempt to describe accurately both the unique properties and the reasons for efficacy of each individual therapeutic interaction.

Medical Care

In the future it seems likely that holistic health centers will continue to grow in number and increase in size, in the kinds of services they provide, and in the variety of providers included. For example, a center that begins with a physician, nurse practitioner, counselor, and biofeedback technician might grow to include physical therapists and massage therapists, acupuncturists, chiropractors, homeopaths, nutritionists, hypnotherapists, and family therapists.

It is also probable that holistic health centers will evolve to provide greater education for more people. They might offer various classes for people with particular kinds of illnesses (diabetes, asthma, cancer, and so forth), offering instruction such as yoga, guided imagery, and relaxation therapies. Lessons in food preparation and herbal and homeopathic remedies might be given. And finally they would provide a forum for mutual support and the solving of individual problems.

It also seems likely that the holistic approach will become more prevalent within hospitals. Therapeutic touch and relaxation therapies can reduce the need for medication and may be able to speed up the healing time after surgery. Why not include them in every ward? Because acupuncture is less dangerous and often more effective than general anesthesia for some surgical procedures, why not use it?

The time is also not far off, I think, when some holistic health centers will attempt to become holistic health maintenance organizations—comprehensive prepaid medical and surgical care programs that are similar in structure to the ones that already exist but that offer a totally different kind of holistic and preventative health care. Perhaps these will be funded by some of the large corporations already sponsoring wellness programs or by a government agency interested in experimenting with a more respectful and potentially less expensive kind of health care. If they prove to be economical as well as appealing and efficient, there is no question that they will become a major force in the health care of the future.

•   •   •   •

CHAPTER 8

. . . .

CHOOSING A HOLISTIC PHYSICIAN

There are several steps to choosing a holistic physician. First, it is important to make sure that the doctor has the appropriate credentials for the treatment he or she is offering—a D.O. or an M.D. is required for physicians. Second, find out what orthodox specialty the doctor is trained in. This may be particularly important if you have a serious or life-threatening condition. A young person with juvenile diabetes will need to work with a holistic physician who is intimately familiar with that illness. Similarly, if you feel your problem is primarily emotional, it will make sense to consult with a holistically oriented psychiatrist. Next, find out something about the complementary techniques that are included in the physician's approach. Is he or she an acupuncturist? A specialist in guided imagery? If you are suffering from a bad back, you will want your physician to be an expert in manipulation, or refer you to someone who is. These questions are important, particularly if the condition for which you are seeking treatment is a serious one. Finally, you should feel comfortable with a physician. Find out the doctor's views on issues that interest or affect you. Most important, determine how honest and open he or she is with you. If a physician seems uninterested in what you have to say, a warning bell should go off.

If you still have questions or doubts, you may want to ask to speak with patients who have seen the physician for years or other doctors who are familiar with his or her work. You may also want to read published articles or office handouts that will inform you about your prospective physician's practice.

If you go through the process of finding and evaluating a physician, you will almost certainly want the help and support of your parents. In the long run, of course, no one else lives inside your body and nobody else can take responsibility for your ongoing health care. But it is enormously helpful to ask advice from people whom you respect, and to have the support of others in adopting the holistic perspective on health by attempting the changes in diet, exercise, behavior, and attitude that may be required. Taking care of your health is not only your responsibility and an opportunity for you to grow and change, but an opportunity for your family to grow and change and learn with you.

•   •   •   •

APPENDIX:

FOR MORE INFORMATION

The following is a list of agencies and organizations that can provide additional information or assistance. The American Osteopathic Association can refer you to osteopathic hospitals and osteopaths in your area.

American Academy of Medical
  Acupuncture
Joseph Helms, M.D.
2520 Milvia Street
Berkeley, CA 94704
(415) 841-7600

American Holistic Medical
  Association/Foundation
2002 Eastlake Ave. East
Seattle, WA 98102
(206) 322-6842

American Holistic Nurses
  Association
205 St. Louis Street, Suite 511
Springfield, MO 65806-1317
(417) 864-5160

American Massage Therapy
  Association
Sally Nieman Pedersberg
National Director of Education
3308 47th Avenue South
Minneapolis, MN 55406

American Medical Students
  Association
Task Force on Humanistic
  Medicine

1890 Preston White Drive
Reston, VA 22091
(703) 620-6600

American Osteopathic Association
212 East Ohio Street
Chicago, IL 60611
(312) 280-5882

American Physical Therapy
  Association
111 North Fairfax Street
Alexandria, VA 22314
(703) 684-2782

Holistic Dental Association
P.O. Box 5007
Durango, CO 81301
(303) 259-6144

National Center for Homeopathy
1500 Massachusetts Avenue, N.W.,
  Suite 41
Washington, DC 20005
(202) 223-6182

FURTHER READING

GENERAL REFERENCES

Boston Women's Health Collective. *Our Bodies, Ourselves.* rev. 2nd ed. New York: Simon & Schuster, 1976. A comprehensive collection of essays on women's health, including specific problems and their appropriate treatment. This is not only an extraordinarily useful book, but a landmark in the self-care movement.

Dychtwald, Ken. *Body-Mind.* New York: Jove, 1978. A good view of some of the connections between the body and mind, this book is particularly helpful in understanding how physical structure reflects emotional problems.

Gordon, James, Dennis Jaffe, and David Bresler. *Mind Body and Health: Toward an Integral Medicine.* New York: Human Sciences Press, 1984. A series of essays on the practice of holistic medicine by a number of distinguished clinicians and researchers.

Grossman, Richard. *The Other Medicines.* New York: Doubleday, 1985. A brief but comprehensive treatment of a number of practices, including acupuncture, homeopathy, yoga, and others. Well-written with useful prescriptions for self-care.

Hastings, Arthur, James Fadiman, and James Gordon. *Health for the Whole Person: The Complete Guide to Holistic Medicine.* Boulder, CO: Westview Press, 1980. An encyclopedic book with more than 30 introductory essays on different aspects of the holistic approach to medicine and an annotated bibliography for each. Extremely useful and an excellent place to start to learn about the subject.

Illich, Ivan. *Medical Nemesis.* New York: Bantam Books, 1977. A very tough, sometimes irritating, but generally thought-provoking critique of some of the excesses and defects of modern medicine.

Kovel, Joel. *A Complete Guide to Therapy*. New York: Pantheon, 1976. A psychiatrist's excellent introduction to modern psychotherapies, including family therapy and humanistic psychology.

Rosenthal, Raymond, and James Gordon. *The Holistic Partnership*. Washington: Aurora, 1984. Four essays on health care including "Health Care in the 80s" and "The Hazards of Medical School."

Rosenthal, Raymond, and James Gordon. *New Directions in Medicine*. Washington: Aurora, 1984. Biographical sketches and descriptions of the medical philosophy and practice of more than 160 innovative health-care professionals with bibliographies for each.

Siegel, Bernie. *Love, Medicine and Miracles*. New York: Harper & Row, 1986. An inspirational book that describes the optimistic practice and the healing approach of Siegel, a surgeon at Yale Medical School. Particularly useful for helping those with serious or chronic illnesses to understand and change self-defeating attitudes.

Weil, Andrew. *Health and Healing*. Cambridge: Houghton Mifflin, 1983. A literate essay detailing Weil's explorations of the philosophy and practice of alternative healing techniques.

ACUPUNCTURE AND MASSAGE

Kaptchuk, T. *The Web That Has No Weaver: Understanding Chinese Medicine*. New York: Congdon and Weed, 1984. A well-written book on the philosophy of acupuncture and how its world-view differs from that of orthodox Western medicine. Particularly helpful in its discussion of pulse diagnosis.

Lindell, Lucinda. *The Book of Massage*. New York: Fireside, 1984. A nice, illustrated introduction to Swedish massage and other therapeutic practices.

MacDonald, Alexander. *Acupuncture: Ancient Art to Modern Medicine*. London: Unwin, 1982. A readable introduction to the traditional theory and practice of acupuncture. If you cannot find it, you may want to consult the following (but more difficult) volume: Mann, Felix. *Acupuncture: The Ancient Chinese Art of Healing and How It Works Scientifically*. New York: Random House, 1971.

FAITH HEALING

Frank, Jerome. *Persuasion and Healing*. New York: Schocken, 1963. A pioneering book that discusses in great detail the importance of faith in healing. Frank also makes an interesting comparison between modern psychotherapists and such primitive healers as witch doctors.

Krieger, Dolores. *The Therapeutic Touch*. Englewood Cliffs, NJ: Prentice-Hall, 1979. An extended discussion of therapeutic touch, the research on which it is based, and the way it is practiced.

HERBALISM

Buchman, Dain. *Herbal Medicine: The Natural Way to Get Well and Stay Well*. New York: Gramercy Publishing Company, 1979. A chatty and useful book on the preparation and utility of different herbs.

Lust, John. *The Herb Book*. New York: Bantam Books, 1974. An excellent and inexpensive compendium of common herbs and the ways to prepare them.

HOMEOPATHY

Cummings, Steven, and Dana Ullman. *Everybody's Guide to Homeopathic Medicines*. Los Angeles: Tarcher, 1984. This useful book discusses the theory and practice of homeopathy, explains homeopathic prescribing, and offers a number of prescriptions for common ailments.

Panos, Maesimund, and Jane Heimlich. *Homeopathic Medicine at Home*. Los Angeles: Tarcher, 1980. A pioneering and extremely useful guide to the home treatment of many common illnesses.

MEDITATION

Goleman, Daniel. *The Varieties of Meditation Experience*. New York: Dutton, 1977. A well-done summary of the various techniques of meditation.

Suzuki, Shumryu. *Zen Mind Beginner's Mind*. New York: Weatherhill, 1970. By the late Zen master, a wonderful guide to developing a meditative mind.

NUTRITION

Ballentine, Rudolph. *Diet and Nutrition: A Holistic Approach*. Honesdale, PA: The Himalayan Institute, 1978. Although some new information in this area has appeared since its publication, this is an extremely comprehensive, useful, and sensible approach to nutrition.

The Editors of *Prevention Magazine*. *The Complete Book of Vitamins*. Emmaus, PA: Rodale Press, 1984. An up-to-date compendium of information about vitamins, minerals, food supplements and their effect on health and disease.

SELF-REGULATION STRATEGIES

Cousins, Norman. *Anatomy of an Illness.* New York: Norton, 1979. The account of how Cousins cured himself of a disabling illness through a mixture of Vitamin C and laughter, respectful medical management, and self-care.

Jaffe, Dennis. *Healing from Within.* New York: Knopf, 1980. A well-written, practical book that details a number of self-regulation strategies.

Pelletier, Kenneth. *Mind as Healer, Mind as Slayer.* New York: Dell, 1978. A comprehensive account of the scientific basis for many self-regulation strategies.

GLOSSARY

acupuncture Chinese system of inserting needles into the body at various, specific points along "energy pathways" called meridians; these points correspond to various internal organs and functions; the insertion of needles is thought to increase or decrease energy, returning the organs to a more harmonious and healthy state

allergy a disorder in the body's immune system in which a person becomes hypersensitive to and creates antibodies against usually neutral particles (allergens) such as dust, pollen, or certain foods; these antibodies (which in most cases are able to destroy the allergen) produce side effects ranging in severity from sneezing or hives to such potentially fatal conditions as anaphylactic shock

alpha wave a type of brain wave that characterizes a state of alert calm; has a frequency of 8 to 11 wave cycles per second

amino acids the building blocks of proteins; of the 20 amino acids found in humans, 10 must be ingested by a person to maintain health; the other 10 can be synthesized by the body

analgesia reduced sensitivity to pain; may result from nerve damage or may be induced with drugs; some practitioners of holistic medicine use hypnosis to induce it

anesthesia loss of sensation, with or without loss of consciousness, in part or all of the body; often induced with drugs to facilitate surgery

antibiotic a substance produced by or derived from a microorganism and able in solution to inhibit or kill another microorganism; used to combat infection

biofeedback the conscious monitoring of information about usually unconscious bodily processes, such as heart rate or blood pressure; can be used to acquire the ability to exert some control over these processes

carbohydrate a member of a group of compounds that share a general biochemical structure comprising carbon, hydrogen, and oxygen; includes sugars and starch; to be metabolized, all types of carbohydrate are broken down into glucose; excess is stored as glycogen or as fat

chiropractic a medical system of physical manipulation based on the belief that certain illnesses are due to inhibited nerve function caused by bone misalignment; similar to osteopathy, but chiropractors do not receive as many years' training as osteopaths

cholesterol a fatlike substance found in blood and tissue; an excess of one type of cholesterol forms deposits on blood-vessel walls that interfere with circulation and are thought to contribute to atherosclerosis, heart disease, and high blood pressure

diabetes (*diabetes mellitus*) a disease in which people are unable to produce the amount of insulin their body requires to metabolize sugar; although predisposition to the disease is genetically determined, other factors, such as obesity or stress, may contribute to its onset

endorphins the body's natural opiates; in addition to having pain-relieving properties, they produce a relaxed feeling of well-being in the body

fasting abstaining from all or most foods for a period of time; done by some people with the intent of "cleansing" their system of toxins thought to accumulate through normal eating or to give their bodies a "rest" from digestion; should never be attempted without a doctor's supervision

fat a substance containing one or more fatty acids; the main substance into which excess carbohydrates are converted for storage by the human body

guided imagery the use of mental images to induce relaxation or help combat a physical problem; possibly a form of hypnosis

hemoglobin the substance in red blood cells that can bind with and carry oxygen to cells and carbon dioxide away from them

herbalism medicinal use of herbs and plants; many common medications are based on ingredients found in plants; herbalists believe that one may benefit from ingesting the active ingredients in the plant form, rather than in the form of synthesized drugs

homeopathy a system of medical treatment based on the idea that "like cures like"; patient is given a very dilute solution of a substance that causes symptoms of his or her disease

hyperactivity a condition mostly affecting children characterized by short attention span, emotional outbursts, and excessive, unnecessary motion; may stem from a genetic defect, a congenital defect, or environmental factors such as poor diet, excess sugar, or lead poisoning; holistic physicians often treat hyperactivity with a special diet

hypnosis a sleeplike state in which one may be open to suggestion or able to experience feelings or memories usually not accessible in a fully conscious state

insulin a hormone that regulates the body's ability to metabolize sugar; used to treat diabetes

macrobiotics an extremely specialized diet usually concentrated on whole grains; thought by some to promote health

massage systematic manipulation of the muscles, joints, and tissues for the purpose of increasing relaxation and for therapeutic reasons; variations of massage techniques are used in some Eastern and European traditions to treat illness and reduce stress

meditation a technique used to bring about a relaxed state somewhat similar to that produced by hypnosis, but without making the person open to suggestion; used as a therapeutic way of improving mental functioning and reducing stress

metabolism the process by which substances within a living organism are chemically broken down in order to release useful energy

mineral a solid, crystalline chemical substance (such as sulfur, salt, or coal) produced by inorganic natural processes; some are necessary to maintain health; often ingested in the form of salts

osteopathy a system of medical treatments based on the belief that physical manipulation of bones and/or muscles can alleviate problems by realigning body parts into their proper positions

phobia an irrationally strong fear of something; e.g., acrophobia is a debilitatingly strong fear of heights

placebo a pill composed of inactive ingredients, sometimes given to patients under the guise of being a medication in order to determine the effectiveness of another medication or to determine whether an illness has a psychological rather than physical cause

progressive muscular relaxation a relaxation technique involving contraction and then relaxation of the muscles

relaxation a generalized lowering of the level of physiological arousal; e.g., lower blood pressure, slower respiratory rate

self-care the practice of taking responsibility for and maintaining a day-to-day balance in one's emotional and physical life in order to stay healthy

self-regulation the deliberate practice of using one's diet, state of mind, exercise, and various medical techniques to cure oneself of an ailment

vitamin one of a group of substances thought to be required by the body but that the body cannot produce

wellness a concept that stresses teaching people how to control their emotions and attitudes in order to feel as well as possible; does not attempt to improve an actual physical condition, but rather to enable one to cope with a condition in a positive manner

INDEX

PICTURE CREDITS

AP/Wide World: pp. 18, 30, 43, 45, 76; Elinor Beckwith/Taurus Photos: p. 54; Susan Berkowitz/Taurus Photos: pp. 29, 31; Bettmann Archive: pp. 17, 47, 63, 71, 72, 74; Laimute Druskis/Taurus Photos: p. 48; Harvard Medical Alumni Bulletin: p. 79; Debra P. Hershkowitz: pp. 23, 61; The Himalayan Institute: pp. 21, 40; Dennis Johnson: p. 13; Eric Kroll/Taurus Photos: pp. 24, 32; John Lehmann/Dr. Benson, Harvard University: p. 97; Alfred Pasieka/Taurus Photos: cover; Karen E. Preuss/Taurus Photos: pp. 86, 91; Martin Rotker/Taurus Photos: p. 33; Shealy Institute for Comprehensive Pain & Health Care: p. 92; Frank Siteman/Taurus Photos; p. 37; UPI/Bettmann Newsphotos: pp. 19, 35, 53, 57, 64, 94, 99; Dr. E. Wineburg/Associated Biofeedback Med. GP: p. 50; Prof. J. R. Worsley/College of Traditional Chinese Acupuncture, U.K.: p. 67; Judy Yoshioka: p. 59; Shirley Zeiberg/Taurus Photos: pp. 27, 38, 82, 101; Original illustrations by Donna Sinisgalli: p. 68; Robin Lazarus: p. 81

James S. Gordon, M.D. , a graduate of Harvard Medical School, practices holistic medicine in Washingon, D.C., and teaches in the departments of psychiatry and community and family medicine at the Georgetown University School of Medicine. For ten years Dr. Gordon was a research psychiatrist at the National Institute of Mental Health, where he was particularly concerned with the development of innovative mental health services for adolescents and their families. He was Director of the Special Study on Alternative Services for President Carter's Commission on Mental Health (1978–79). For six years, he was on the Board of Trustees of the American Holistic Medical Association. He has also served as chief of the adolescent service of St. Elizabeth's Hospital in Washington, D.C. Dr. Gordon is the author of more than 100 articles and author or editor of seven previous books including the award-winning *Health for the Whole Person: The Complete Guide to Holistic Medicine, New Directions in Medicine,* and *The Healing Partnership.*

Dale C. Garell, M.D., is medical director of California Children Services, Department of Health Services, County of Los Angeles. He is also associate dean for curriculum at the University of Southern California School of Medicine and clinical professor in the Department of Pediatrics & Family Medicine at the University of Southern California School of Medicine. From 1963 to 1974, he was medical director of the Division of Adolescent Medicine at Children's Hospital in Los Angeles. Dr. Garell has served as president of the Society for Adolescent Medicine, chairman of the youth committee of the American Academy of Pediatrics, and as a forum member of the White House Conference on Children (1970) and White House Conference on Youth (1971). He has also been a member of the editorial board of the *American Journal of Diseases of Children.*

C. Everett Koop, M.D., Sc.D., is Surgeon General, Deputy Assistant Secretary for Health, and Director of the Office of International Health of the U.S. Public Health Service. A pediatric surgeon with an international reputation, he was previously surgeon-in-chief of Children's Hospital of Philadelphia and professor of pediatric surgery and pediatrics at the University of Pennsylvania. Dr. Koop is the author of more than 175 articles and books on the practice of medicine. He has served as surgery editor of the *Journal of Clinical Pediatrics* and editor-in-chief of the *Journal of Pediatric Surgery.* Dr. Koop has received nine honorary degrees and numerous other awards, including the Denis Brown Gold Medal of the British Association of Paediatric Surgeons, the William E. Ladd Gold Medal of the American Academy of Pediatrics, and the Copernicus Medal of the Surgical Society of Poland. He is a Chevalier of the French Legion of Honor and a member of the Royal College of Surgeons, London.

S
San Rafael, CA 94901